BLACK ELEGIES

ON SEEING

Black Elegies: Meditations on the Art of Mourning, Kimberly Juanita Brown, 2025

Mortevivum: Photography and the Politics of the Visual, Kimberly Juanita Brown, 2024

BLACK ELEGIES

MEDITATIONS ON THE ART OF MOURNING

KIMBERLY JUANITA BROWN

BROWN UNIVERSITY DIGITAL PUBLICATIONS
PROVIDENCE, RHODE ISLAND

THE MIT PRESS
CAMBRIDGE, MASSACHUSETTS
LONDON, ENGLAND

Please scan this QR code to find an open access digital edition of *Black Elegies*.

This publication has been supported by the MIT Press Grant Program for Diverse Voices and the Fund for Diverse Voices.

The MIT Press would like to thank the anonymous peer reviewers who provided comments on drafts of this book. The generous work of academic experts is essential for establishing the authority and quality of our publications. We acknowledge with gratitude the contributions of these otherwise uncredited readers.

This book was set in Halyard Text by Jen Jackowitz. Printed and bound in the United States of America.

Library of Congress Cataloging-in-Publication Data

Names: Brown, Kimberly Juanita, 1972- author.
Title: Black elegies: meditations on the art of mourning / Kimberly Juanita Brown.
Description: Providence, Rhode Island : Brown University Digital Publications ; Cambridge Massachusetts : The MIT Press, 2025. | Series: On seeing ; 2 | Includes bibliographical references and index.
Identifiers: LCCN 2024017206 (print) | LCCN 2024017207 (ebook) | ISBN 9780262551724 (paperback) | ISBN 9780262382427 (pdf) | ISBN 9780262382434 (epub)
Subjects: LC SH: American poetry—African American authors—History and criticism. | Elegiac poetry, American—History and criticism. | LCGFT: Literary criticism.
Classification: LCC PS310.B53 B76 2025 (print) | LCC PS310.B53 (ebook) | DDC 811/.5409896073—dc23/eng/20240829
LC record available at https://lccn.loc.gov/2024017206
LC ebook record available at https://lccn.loc.gov/2024017207

10 9 8 7 6 5 4 3 2 1

For us

Heavy. . . . This place
is heavy.

—Toni Morrison

CONTENTS

SERIES FOREWORD

Visual culture has always been central to meaning making and most recently technology has catapulted its global stakes. Today there is greater access and exposure to visual culture than ever before, outpacing our ability to reflect upon its implications. In response to the need for diverse perspectives on the growing impact of visual culture, the MIT Press began work on a new book series in 2018. Conceived over several years of research and intensive discussion with international scholars, the On Seeing series emerged with a commitment to increase visual literacy.

In 2022, the MIT Press and Brown University Digital Publications announced a partnership to launch the series with inclusivity and access as driving motivations. Books in the On Seeing visual culture series are published in print and open access, media-rich digital editions to serve the widest possible audience.

Defined by rigorous research, bold positions, and cultural relevance, On Seeing publications shape new conversations about how we see, comprehend, and participate in visual culture, and how we can do so with informed agency. The diverse authors of On Seeing investigate the ways that power relations are inscribed in the visual and they develop knowledge about how what we see—and what remains hidden from view—is related to justice.

INTRODUCTION: GRIEF IN THE ATMOSPHERE

An obituary is for the public, a lament is for the community.
—Teju Cole

Out of the darkness, up from the ground, bodies draped in earth tones, move. Slowly, with arms outstretched, they reach up, hands open: an offering, a prayer, an archive, an elegy. Alvin Ailey's ballet *Revelations* brings African American culture through its meditative and linear history, affixed to the music that has instrumentalized black life in the reservoir of the larger world. For Thomas DeFrantz, "This image of bodies rooted to the floor while faces are directed upward confirms a choreographic motif of split focus that permeates the dance. These are people in physical bondage invoking, though their movements, spiritual deliverance."[1] The spirituals that wrap and lace *Revelations* do so through black church familiarity and sonic potency. Beginning with "I Been 'Buked and I've Been Scorned" and "Didn't My Lord Deliver Daniel," "Wade in the Water," "I Wanna Be Ready" and ending with the boisterous "Rocka My Soul (in the Bosom of Abraham)," *Revelations* "began as a staged enactment of the choral singing of spirituals."[2] Thinking of *Revelations* in this way, as movement through the recesses of enslaved mourning and music, gives the performance its requisite gravity. With a pitch-black background, dancers of different shades assemble in unison, spinning out through portals of collective interiority and exhibiting the multifaceted enactments of forced improvisation.

Revelations is performed in three sections: "Pilgrim of Sorrow," "Take Me to the Water," and "Move, Members, Move." Each section marks a distinct moment in African American history from enslavement to religious salvation and freedom of movement. Ailey's choreography encompasses angular movement with wide jumps and expressive, muscular gestures. The performance exemplifies bodily stamina and grace, resilience, beauty, and the elegance of purpose, what Ailey referred to as his "blood memories."[3] *Blood memories* are born with you, are born *in* you, and set your directional body dial in the arena of creative extraction that falls under your control.

Sorrow songs, or spirituals, are one such illustration of the cultural production of forced improvisation. Like other manifestations of black art originating with captives from the transatlantic slave trade, sorrow songs developed as expressive sonic venues of release for black subjects, holding the horrors of the experience together with motifs of survival. Improvisatory in its construction, "Antiphony (call and response)," according to Paul Gilroy, "is the principal formal feature of these musical traditions. It has come to be seen as a bridge from music into other modes of cultural expression, supplying, along with improvisation, montage, and dramaturgy, the hermeneutic keys to the full medley of black artistic practices."[4] *Revelations* offers this "full medley" in mournful lows and spiritual highs, in a measured hint of corporeal retrieval that reckons with losses so expansive and violent that it would take land and ocean to begin to navigate its breadth. Its reach.

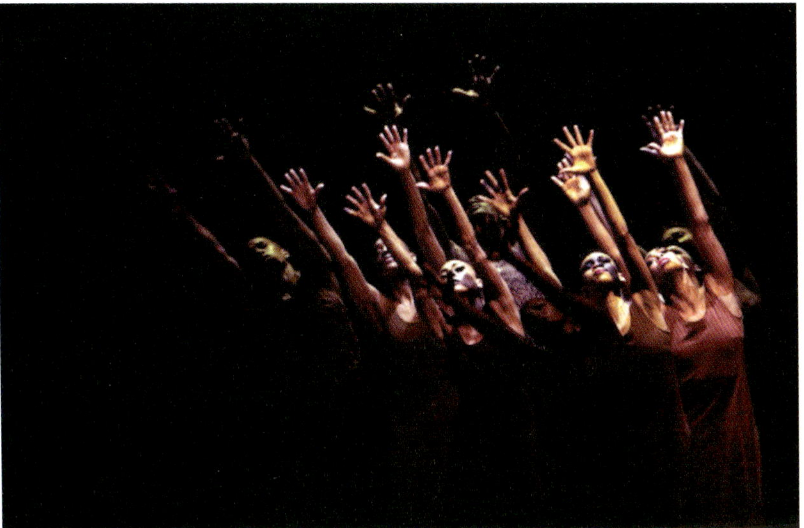

Figure 0.1
Alvin Ailey's *Revelations*. Courtesy of Getty Images.

John Coltrane's masterpiece *A Love Supreme* is an all-consuming sonic conjuring that trips over the frame of four suites in thirty-two minutes and forty-seven seconds. *A Love Supreme* is spiritual transcendence, the arc of human existence, a love story, an elegy. Like the brilliant architecture of a jazz monument to God, Coltrane exceeds the boundaries of what is possible musically, materially. In four stages of sonic evolution, the listener is treated to the four planes of Coltrane's movement: Acknowledgement, Resolution, Pursuance, and Psalm. These nuanced stages of black ecstasy and black grief end in the repetition of a chant of survival: a conjuring of the sort that inspires, redeems, anchors, and retrieves. *A love supreme . . . a love supreme . . .*

Of all the jazz musicians emerging out of the U.S. South in the 1930s, 1940s, and 1950s, Coltrane is the one most steeped in the cloak of grief, cloaked in an understanding of loss, longing, and black retrieval. "Sound is not ideologically neutral," Ren Ellis Neyra writes. "Sound manifests in the shapes made in captivity, and from bodies that exceed the state's self-sovereign and antiblack epistemologies."[5] Coltrane exceeds the frame of sound shapes made within and beyond captivity, in the outer reaches of black embodiment that metaphysically command a place at the table where grief also resides. "In all jazz, and especially in the blues," James Baldwin writes, "there is something tart and ironic, authoritative and double-edged . . . only people who have been 'down the line,' as the song puts it, know what this music is about."[6] The music, as Coltrane imagines it, as he performed and deployed it, is about mourning. And the ghostly matters that lead to mourning as a form of release. Coltrane was in a meditative and contemplative space when he created *A Love Supreme*. Elliott H. Powell notes that "Coltrane's iteration of the other side of things involves addressing life events of the present (e.g., sadness) and transforming them for a better future world (e.g., happiness)."[7] What Powell refers to as Coltrane's "queer sonic eccentricity" is connected to James Baldwin's auditory retrievals. In both men, the cadence of grief was ever present, and constantly connected to their way of moving though the world.

In Baldwin's first published nonfiction book *Notes of a Native Son*, the title essay appears in the center of the text as the author guides the reader through his processes of mourning while engaging in the difficult work of being black in America and beyond its borders. Published in 1955, *Notes* is Baldwin in his narrative arc, composed of ten essays that range from literary and film criticism to his personal thoughts on his evolution as an African American writer born and raised in New York City. The essay "Notes of a Native Son" begins with the catastrophic convergence of Baldwin's father succumbing to illness on the same day that Baldwin's sibling is born. Further, Baldwin tells us, "The day of my father's funeral had also been my nineteenth birthday," marking life, death,

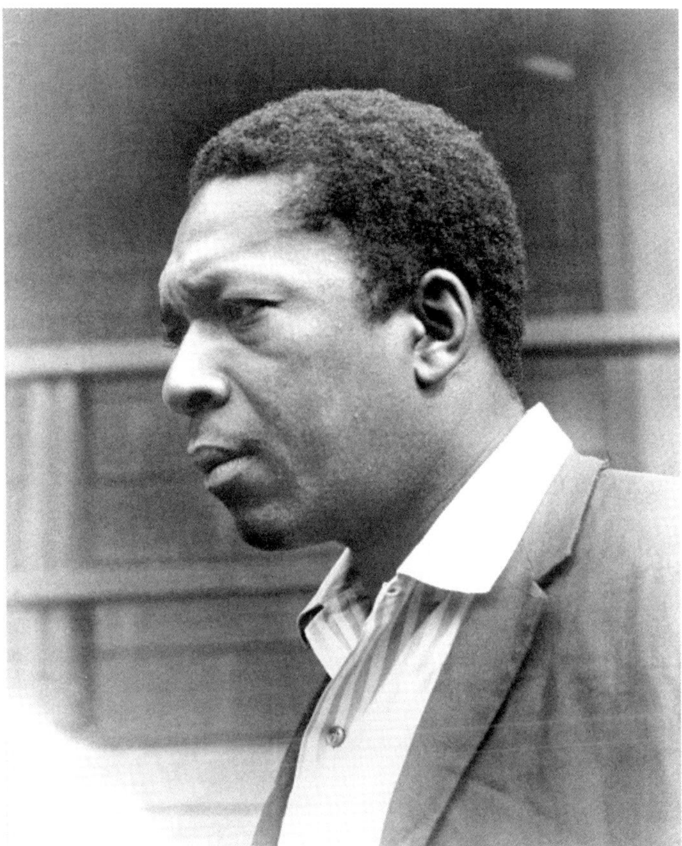

Figure 0.2
John Coltrane, cover photograph for *A Love Supreme*. Michael Ochs Archive, courtesy of Getty Images.

and renewal in the same space where he grapples with all the restrictions on his humanity that he has experienced in his short time on earth.[8] Of his father Baldwin writes, "He had lived and died in an intolerable bitterness of spirit and it frightened me . . . to see how powerful and overflowing this bitterness could be and to realize this bitterness was now mine."[9] As we know, Baldwin was able to delve into the difficult intricacies of emotion with the precision of a surgeon. But I think we fail to consider all this cost him, even as his writings offered the world a path through the steel portals of rage and grief that often stalk black life. "The dead man mattered," Baldwin declares at the end of his "Notes of a Native Son" essay. "The new life mattered; blackness and whiteness did not matter; to believe that they did was to acquiesce in one's own destruction."[10] In all the ways that matter, Baldwin used his voice to hold in regard that which could easily be lost in the hierarchy of cultural refusals and racial animus. Attuned as he was to the cadence and rhythm of black life, Baldwin's profound gifts were held in place in order to keep black people alive and offer some solace to those lost. "I can't be a pessimist," he says in a clip from director Raoul Peck's recent film *I Am Not Your Negro*, "because I'm alive." Baldwin continues, "To be a pessimist means that you have agreed that human life is an academic matter. So I'm forced to be an optimist. I am forced to believe that we can survive whatever we must survive."[11] In a series of essays and interviews, in a four-part jazz tribute, or a dance performance marking the trajectory from captivity to freedom, black elegies are everywhere. In this book I want to consider artistic representations of black grief as part of the extended discourse of the poetic elegy, telling us something about meditations of loss. In these instances of elegiac deployment, it is within the atmosphere of national refusal and dispossession that artists and writers do the scaffolding work of mourning while black. Part of this scaffolding work includes imagining spaces for grief where it might be possible to acknowledge the violence that attends black life.

Mary Lee Bendolph, one of the famous Gee's Bend quilters from Alabama, is known for her sophisticated and elegant quilts. Bendolph created *Ghost Pockets* from her husband Rubin Bendolph's old clothing. Created in 2003, ten years after Rubin's passing, *Ghost Pockets* is Bendolph's way of holding Rubin close—close enough to touch—with strips of clothing

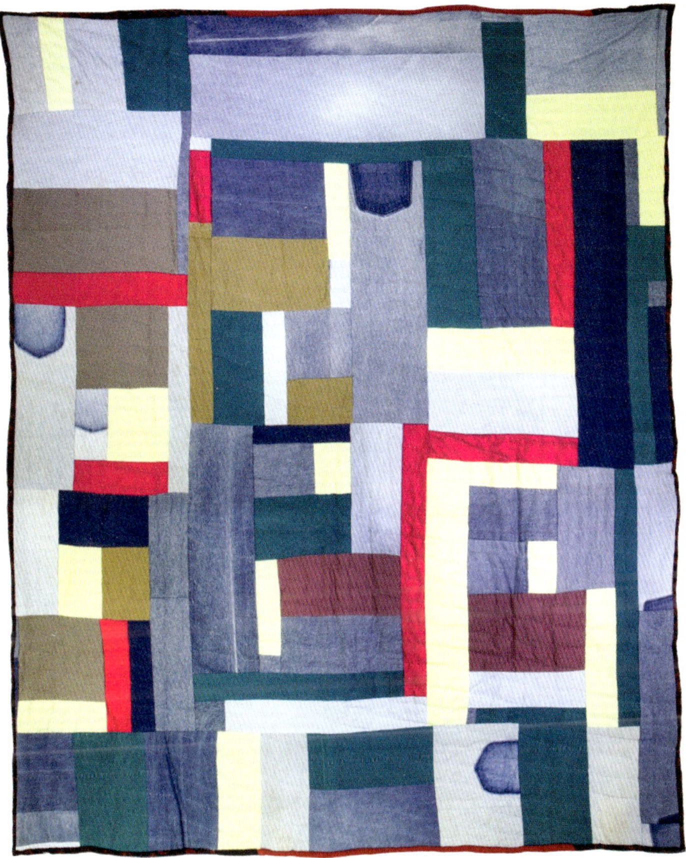

Figure 0.3
Mary Lee Bendolph (American, born 1935), *Ghost Pockets*, 2003. Mixed fabrics including denim, cotton, polyester, and synthetic wool. Purchased with the Art Acquisition Endowment Fund. Mount Holyoke College Art Museum, South Hadley, Massachusetts. Photograph by Laura Shea.

he wore when he was alive. With the deepened indigo outlines (the ghosts) of denim pockets as markers, *Ghost Pockets* displays lines of red with bursts of yellow, purple, and gray. The quilt deploys a haptic materiality, which soothes and consoles, all with the tactile consistency of touch. African American quilt traditions emerged during and after slavery, when enslaved workers would collect scraps of discarded fabric used to make clothing and stitch them together in order to craft a bedcover/ blanket to keep warm in the colder months. This particular form of utilitarian improvisation has led to an art practice that involves geometric abstract design alongside bold strips of color. *Ghost Pockets* is imbued with a painterly inheritance while participating in the mourning processes of black grief. The importance of creating a tactile object of memory making, one that highlights the retention of the person remembered, is connected through the stitching in a visual display of sporadic ghost pockets that serve as reminders of that which was lost. Elegies direct the line of communication from the living to the dead and back again. They take many forms. "I don't believe in ghosts," Tiya Miles writes. "Not really, not rationally. But this did not stop me, on a damp winter night in 2012, from going in search of one."[12] I, too, am on a search for ghosts, or at least the haunting residue of their presence. To be a researcher of transatlantic slavery leaves one few alternatives than to travel among ghosts wherever they take you. I visited my first slave plantation in 2010, and it was Thomas Jefferson's Monticello. The ghosts there haunted me, have stayed with me ever since.

My first trip to Monticello was a solo journey. And it was harder than I even imagined it would be. I remember sitting on one of the benches on the property after the tour and feeling the heaviness of the space, even while I was surrounded by a kind of boundless admiration for Jefferson that did not fit the gravity of what I was experiencing. I was also the only black person on the tour, which was surprising to me. There were awkward glances from other visitors to the plantation, as if the only thing standing between them and their enthusiasm for the property was my dark brown body signaling a link to enslavement. The second time I convinced my friend Shirley to accompany me from New York to Virginia so that I was

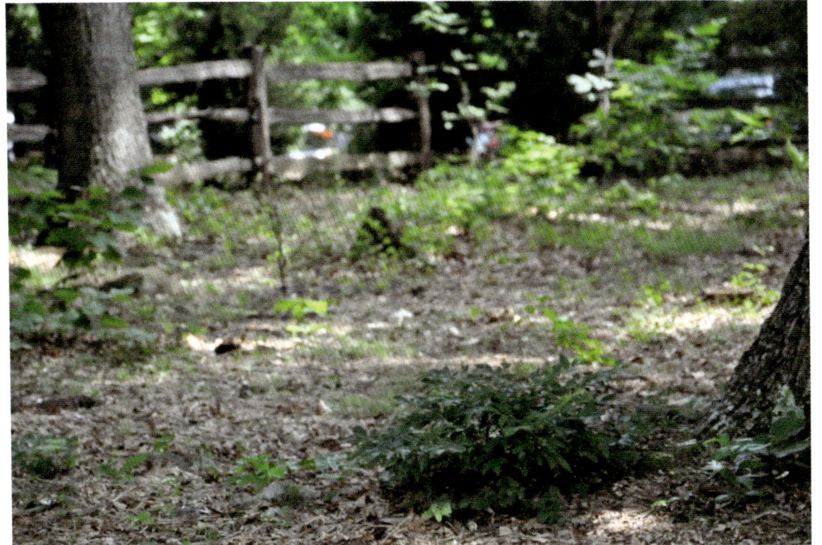

Figure 0.4
African American graveyard, Monticello.

not alone. The third time I visited the plantation I brought my friend Vanessa as a witness. By my third visit to Monticello, I was deliberately looking for ghosts—or at least my own personal haunting.

Ghosts occupy space and time, requiring our attention. In fact, depending on where you are you may be directed by one, and ordered to do its bidding. Perhaps what the ghost wants is recognition, perhaps vengeance, and maybe even a little bit of their own grief to carry. A ghost who wants nothing does not exist. Think of it that way. To enter a time and space—a room—a park—a temple of worship—an alleyway, is to confront the *there* that came before you. An ancestor, a kindred spirit. To speak to you and often through you, so that you are in communion with the living and the dead while you are here. We could call it purposeful synesthesia.

To enter a time and space—a room—a park—a temple of worship—an alleyway, is to confront the *there* that came before you.

"I don't believe I am synesthetic," Teju Cole writes. "But I cannot always account for the intensity of my sensations."[13] Synesthesia, as Cole describes it, is a way of navigating multiple sensory experiences simultaneously. Black cultural productions privilege a heightened relationship to the sensorial, often enacting a deepened feeling as part of the process. *Black Elegies* is attuned to the subtle overlap of the sensorial that is imbued with immersive properties of sight, sound, taste, and touch. This subtle overlap is the interest of this book, and so I have chosen texts that exceed the frame of their emergence to tell us something about what happens in that overflow. Texts like *Revelations* enact a kind of mirage of feeling that goes beyond mere performance to expose something new, something elongated and inscribed. Some of the choices I make here illustrate my way of seeing and feeling, and therefore emerge from my particular vantage point. I hope you move with me as I make sense of my choices along the way. My mandate has been simple: If I think it is an elegy, then I pursue this possibility, and I follow the winding road to see where it may take me. I ask that you take this ride with me in the hope that we may find communion in the arc of creative intention before us. In this way, sight is a visual navigation that arrives to inform the haptic, and sound is a way to see beyond the delineations of discovery most immediately available for subjective experience. Black elegies, then, employ a poetics of the sensorial that indexes and archives the synesthetic potency of the form. My aim is to use a poetics of loss to manage the canyon of beauty and grief in multimodal forms of elegiac expression.

This book is one way to commune with ghosts—of nations, people, histories, and the past. It is a weaving of examinations of fiction, film, poetry, and photography. It depends heavily on the musicality of longing and loss. It flows, like water with "perfect memory" from one purposeful expression of grief to another.[14] "We die," Toni Morrison writes in her Nobel Prize-winning speech. "That may be the meaning of life. But we *do* language," she continues. "That may be the measure of our lives."[15] Black elegies tarry where statistics skew precision of loss, where slippages between there and here expose the fallacy of temporality. "Sometimes we summon our ghosts; sometimes our ghosts are a constitutive part of ourselves," Habiba Ibrahim writes. "At other times, our ghosts lovingly pursue us, and lovingly unmake us."[16] For what is a ghost story but a way to see into the abyss of what is already there? So conjured, so called. Be they duppy, banshee, ghost, or haint, they signal the thing that remains after loss: people, land, country, or culture. They demand that we give space for grief or they will take it without permission, like a momentary wind knocked out of you as you travel along your day.

(After the murder, after the burial)
Emmett's mother is a pretty-faced thing;
the tint of pulled taffy.
She sits in a red room,
drinking black coffee.
She kisses her killed boy.
And she is sorry.
Chaos in windy grays
through a red prairie.

A quatrain reminds the reader of the lift that rhyme can bring to poetry. This one, from Gwendolyn Brooks's poem "The Last Quatrain of the Ballad of Emmett Till," upends this expectation.[17] To the promise of musicality embedded in the ballad, Brooks mutes this lift so that it lands in elegy. So that it does the work required of grief in the dark, where somber tones tell another story. Did the directional pull of black elegies have to find another way? Did the demands of opacity dictate the terms of engagement? Did black lives find a way to redress the needs of an ever-expansive collective? Part four of Coltrane's *A Love Supreme*, Psalm, meanders around his tenor sax, what Michael S. Harper refers to as "the tenor kiss, tenor love," stretching out the length of the section like a lover yearning for the lost touch of the beloved.[18] Or the pinnacle of glory that prayer and practice have held out as a promise to the initiated. "Emmett's mother is a pretty-faced thing; / the tint of pulled taffy. / She sits in a red room, / drinking black coffee. / She kisses her killed boy. / And she is sorry. / Chaos in windy grays / through a red prairie."[19] Brooks weaves a sonic quatrain out of images of sharp color that define Mamie Till's mourning process as she seeks justice for "her killed boy." The poet lets us into the arena of longing as it is tethered to a Chicago mother's grief for the son violently taken during a summer spent with relatives down south. Till is not the first child taken with such violent intention in the United States or beyond and he will not be the last.

When Carrie Mae Weems creates a series of silkscreened panels, each featuring the name and statistical details of those black subjects killed by law enforcement officers, she couples the information with archival pigment prints swathed in deep blue. These ghostly figures haunt the frame as they exceed it, drawing out the navigation of racial violence though the multiple bodies it will claim. The images themselves are mesmerizing, not simply due to Weems's stunning atmospheric control, but also due to the momentary (and lingering) iteration of familiarity in each of the frames. We both know and can never know these people. This familiarity haunts, because in large part what we encounter is the fading image of a black subject not fully seen, but assumed, dismissed, surveilled, and redacted. Blurred blue and out of focus, Weems has rendered them unavailable for capture, made visually poignant since the viewer gets to participate in their temporal escape. Figures both present and absent, real and imagined, captured and fugitive. In the thickened blue that absorbs and releases them, Weems has created haptic possibility. Images more tethered to touch than sight, and distributed visually as still images in movement, in mourning.

Weems's recent series *Slow Fade to Black* offers an earlier precursor to *The Usual Suspects*. In *Slow Fade to Black* Weems blurs images of iconic black stars of stage and screen, placing

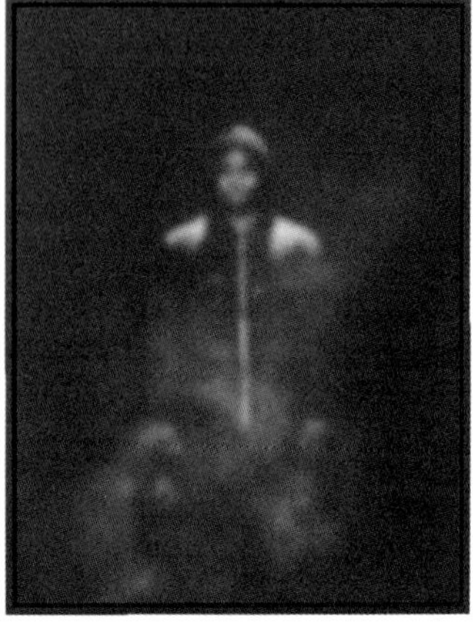

Figure 0.5
Carrie Mae Weems, *All the Boys (Profile 1)*, 2016. © Carrie Mae Weems. Courtesy of the artist and Gladstone Gallery, New York, Fraenkel Gallery, San Francisco, and Galerie Barbara Thumm, Berlin.

them out of focus and into a kind of blurred anonymity. This blurred anonymity in turn is a kind of elegy, for it allows the viewer to contemplate the full measure of access and visual aggression that stalked women from Billie Holiday to Katherine Dunham, Mahalia Jackson, and Nina Simone. As each woman is exposed to the gaze of the viewer, they are simultaneously rendered unavailable for such scrutiny, leaving only a hint of their visual availability behind. *The Usual Suspects* removes clean visual availability in favor of a thick, blue immersive engagement that is at once haunting and familiar. This project moves between the haunting and the familiar, choosing to illuminate the wonder located there. In this, I trust the reader may also engage in discoveries, which, like a strip of bright red in a field of gray may surprise and delight, settle and soothe. Like a ghostly sorrow song with a double meaning or a photograph gloriously presented large and bold, but out

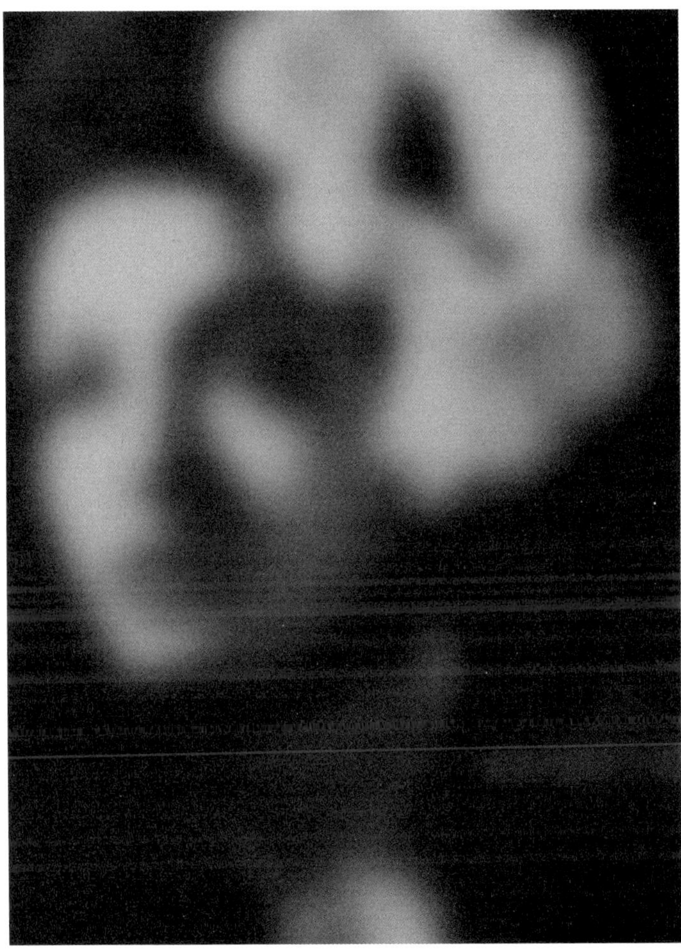

Figure 0.6
Carrie Mae Weems, *Slow Fade to Black (Billie Holiday)*. © Carrie Mae Weems. Courtesy of the artist and Gladstone Gallery, New York, Fraenkel Gallery, San Francisco, and Galerie Barbara Thumm, Berlin.

of focus. These ghosts, with their demands and commands, open sensorial capacities so that layering or conflation can occur, leading to something like ecstasy. An ecstatic retrieval where sight, sound, smell, and touch are heightened so that an immersive experience consumes the body, leaving it susceptible to the encounter to come.

There are constitutive elements in the manner of black grief we must grapple with. When I specify "black grief" I am thinking about an enclosure of blackness that must continually resist the violent atmospheric presence of antiblackness. Christina Sharpe writes, "Anti-blackness is pervasive *as* climate. The weather necessitates changeability and improvisation; it is the atmospheric condition of time and place; it produces new ecologies. . . . When the only certainty is the weather that produces a pervasive climate of anti-blackness, what must we know in order to move through these environments in which the push is always toward Black death?"[20] Sharpe's investigation of the heavy burden placed on black subjects takes into account the many ways that black life has resisted and continues to resist the violence of antiblackness.

So, along with all the ways that black subjects live and die, there are the sensational and arbitrary acts of extreme violence that spectacularize death in ways that do not allow for the dignity of grieving, privately or otherwise, without hypervigilance on the part of the survivors. Survivors are my investment with *Black Elegies*, not just those who have survived a loved one who has passed on, but also survivors who negotiate losses that do not end in death: losses like distance, homeland, diminishment, and the absence of care that often accompanies racialized subjects everywhere they go.

And they go. Carried by histories and memories that frame their relationships, connections, and ways of being in the world. They move, like ripples on still water, marking place and subtly changing the elements around them. They grieve, seen or unseen in the light of day or the dark of night. They create, in the vibrancy of human experience and spiritual will. What if we paused to spend time with the gravity of these gestures? What if we were to hold them close, like a love object in an unfolding scene sutured to black life?

BLACK ART, BLACK GRIEF

Dawoud Bey's *Elegy* conjoins ghosts and atmosphere in a series of black-and-white photographs that bring black grief into stark visibility. A mixture of portraits and landscapes, the images range in meditative potency while surprising the viewer with flecks of presence, of place. In binding people to land, to foliage, and to the aquatic, Bey simplifies the understanding of black American culture so that it emerges from the ground (with indigenous recognition) and flows outward on bodies of water headed nowhere. Headed everywhere. A mixture of earlier and more recent works, *Elegy* is Bey's love poem to black aliveness, to black survival, black memory and longevity. His 2017 gelatin silver print *Untitled (Lake Erie and Sky)* is a line on the horizon bringing the heavens to the brim of Lake Erie to tell a different kind of ghost story. Something foreboding this way comes, as viewers are entangled in a web of recognition that demands stasis. You are to take your time here. That is the demand. There is no way to quickly disperse a ghost.

Steve McQueen's 2015 photograph *Lynching Tree* is a seemingly innocuous tree set deep in a Louisiana forest. McQueen found the tree while scouting locations for the 2013 film he directed, *12 Years a Slave*. The tree's overgrowth hides the bodies of victims of lynching in the enclosure of its own foliage. Like water sanitizing a crime scene. The fraught relationship between black subjects and the land that sustains and often claims them is McQueen's visual concern. And in the way that the land makes those claims, people have natal stories that tether them to place, giving them a sense of history, family, legacy, and continuity. Haunting in its anonymity, the lynching tree nevertheless indexes its horror, since any tree, north to south, east to west, can be utilized as a violent framework of subjection. Its gestural composure allows for both possibilities to exist in the same place and time: peace and horror.

Ebony G. Patterson's 2018 *Three Kings Weep* produces this duality in a video triptych featuring three finely clothed and bejeweled black men moving in slow motion. The three-channel video projection allows the viewer to hold the men in their gaze as they slowly remove layer after layer of clothing while tears well up in their eyes. *Three Kings Weep* is overlaid with references to Claude McKay's famous poem "If We Must Die." The intensity of the gaze combines with raw vulnerability wherein the men cry openly while not averting that gaze.

Visual art as memorial, as elegy, traverses the world of the living and the dead, the grieving and those to be grieved. In this suture between the loved and the mourned, grief coheres around the palpable recognition of existence that is held in place.

Curator Okwui Enwezor's *Grief and Grievance: Art and Mourning in America* exhibition addressed what he called "the crystallization of black grief in the face of a politically orchestrated white grievance," as one way the 2016 U.S. presidential election marked a "commitment to white supremacy." Before his untimely death in 2019, Enwezor put together this exhibition and catalog examining "modes of representation in different mediums where artists have addressed the concept of mourning, commemoration, and loss as a direct response to the national emergency of black grief."[21] Black grief as a national emergency is an alteration from previous discourses on black life or black death. The indifference that meets black subjectivity, the hypervisibility and surveillance, reinforce the disposability of black subjects in a contemporary visual framework. It is with Enwezor's prompt that I want to consider "the national emergency of black grief" as a way to attend to mourning practices in art and literature that engage the discourse of elegy both within and beyond the genre of poetry.

In this suture between the loved and the mourned, grief coheres around the palpable recognition of existence that is held in place.

Somewhere along the way to completing my latest book project it occurred to me that I was in the process of writing two books. *Mortevivum: Photography and the Politics of the Visual* concerns the relationship between documentary photography and histories of antiblackness. For *Mortevivum* I examine images of the dead and dying in the media in order to measure the space of visual possibility foreclosed for black subjects on the cusp of the twenty-first century. *Black Elegies* contemplates sites of mourning that do not register immediately as archives of grief: the landscape of southern U.S. slave plantations, a spontaneous street performance, a quilt constructed out of the clothing worn by a loved one, a ballet to hold the memory of black history, an aeolian harp installed at an institute of European art.

Here, in the repetitious refrain of the sorrow song, in its current alteration and temporal elongation, it cannot be appropriated for whom it is not intended. For a circular formation modulates, with incredible vocal control, the cavernous wall of grief that is black. Without a nod to the universal. Resonance. Vibration. Reverberation. Echo. In the full embodiment of this rendition of the sorrow song/ spiritual "Motherless Chil'" by Sweet Honey in the Rock we hear the amplified extension of the mournful loss of the familial illustrated in so many works of the black diaspora. I want to think through the sonic life of *Black Elegies* here, with a few thoughts about the cadence and order of slavery's perpetual haunting, its unyielding and generational lament. "Motherless Chil'" is, for me at least, of the thousands of sorrow songs written, sung, and reproduced by unnamed and uncredited slaves in the United States, one that emphasized the distance between over there and over here. That profoundly violent and repetitive extraction of children from their mothers gave slavery a cruelty beyond human calculation and a horrifyingly corporeal precision. "The most universal definition of the slave is a stranger," Saidiya Hartman writes in *Lose Your Mother*. "Torn from kin and community, exiled from one's country, dishonored and violated, the slave defines the position of the outsider."[22] In this a cappella version of the popular sorrow song "Motherless Chil" by Sweet Honey in the Rock, arranged and with lead vocals by Carol Maillard, slight alterations in the lyrics extend the discourse of slavery and motherloss beyond the boundary marker of slavery's extended geography. Black subjects must both cross the ocean and also somehow embody it. They must reproduce and *be* reproducible. They must labor without an end on the horizon. And what they create will be taken from them. Though they represent the profound loss of the motherless child and its natural corollary, the childless mother, they alone live with the trauma of this event. And they must do all of this within a very limited rubric of possible release. And therein lies the vibration. The resonance. The echo. The reverberation. The repetition. And the call. Sight, sound, and touch extend the trauma of the Middle Passage beyond the bodies and the territories it encompassed. For those who made the journey are dispersed and not often remembered. They labor and love "a long way from home" and negotiate the sliver of space between over here and back there. Sorrow songs provide the guidepost to the elegies explored in this book. They appear as a particularly American genre, coming from enslaved workers on plantations in the U.S. South. That we have thousands of spirituals preserved from the nineteenth century speaks to the horrors of slavery in the United States as well as the efforts put forward to create something beautiful out of the devastation this has caused.

OF ELEGIES

Within the genre of poetry dedicated to addressing the depth and breadth of loss, the elegy has a long and vibrant history, particularly in the United States. Black elegies, though, have a less secure space in American literature. In a problematic racial canon that often takes mourning as a white presentation, elegies are often bereft of black poetry but full of a poetics of black mourning. For instance, the cover image of Max Cavitch's book

American Elegy: The Poetry of Mourning from the Puritans to Whitman features a photograph of African American twin boys, one of whom is dead. In the visual dissonance of the cover image we can see the process of black elegiac refusal at work, as a book of literary criticism that has almost no mention of black grief utilizes an image of palpable black loss as its central visual symbol. Black twins, one living, one dead, both offered up as objects of emotion, not for themselves, but to assist in the expression of (assumed) white grievers. How did African Americans become located outside processes of mourning readily available to others? What is there to understand in the refusal to acknowledge the existence of black grief? *Black Elegies* considers the expansive range of cultural productions that move in sight, sound, and touch, like sorrow songs with double meanings. My project coheres around the concept of *elongated grief* that is the residue of trauma African Americans and other diasporic subjects experience due to the history of slavery, empire, and racial violence in the nation and beyond its borders. This history of violence necessitates multivalent approaches to the properties of mourning that assist in alleviating some of the pain of existing while black.

Elongated grief may look like a fictional narrative about a pregnant film actress whose body cannot sustain the life held within her, because she has reached the end of a violent horizon with no end in sight. It may look like a cinematic exchange where the gaze enraptures its protagonists as if letting go would be the end of everything they know. It might sound like an instrumental accompaniment to a eulogy for girls killed in a church explosion. Or it could feel like the unfinished manuscript by a writer who was never at a loss for words. *Black Elegies* moves with and beyond disparate iterations of artistic mourning to uncover the deepened frequencies of loss, as that which is discernible is not always all that is there.

Chapter 1 of *Black Elegies*, "Sight," deploys the visual to access avenues of recognition that allow black subjects to

Black Elegies considers the expansive range of cultural productions that move in sight, sound, and touch, like sorrow songs with double meanings.

envision processes of mourning as inclusive of the gaze. I'm interested in works that grapple with the space between visuality, loss, and subjectivity. In this case the gaze is a way to regard from a place of mutual understanding. Chapter 1 features work from Roy DeCarava, Jesmyn Ward, Alvin Ailey / Judith Jamison, Toby Sisson, Toni Cade Bambara, Jeannette Ehlers, and Toni Morrison. Chapter 2, "Sound," relates to the relationship between black mourning and the sonic. Black sonic practices range from sorrow songs and sermons, to film renditions, fiction, and poetry. Chapter 2 concerns the sonic life of loss and includes works by Kahlil Joseph, Vievee Francis, Jennie C. Jones, Marvin Gaye, Amanda Russhell Wallace, and Saidiya Hartman. Chapter 3, "Touch," engages the haptic gravitational pull of touch that creates its own enclosure of catharsis, moving from one bereaved black subject to another. Chapter 3 examines works from Toni Morrison, Dell Marie Hamilton, Carl Phillips, Barry Jenkins, Audre Lorde, Rebecca Hall, and Michelle Cliff.

I am purposely resisting the desire to encapsulate black mourning processes around Sigmund Freud's important essay "Mourning and Melancholia," since his meditation on the contours of grief cannot be easily grafted onto black diasporic subjects whose profound losses precede Freud's intervention by two hundred years and continue still. I am asking different questions for this book project. A constant question that circulates around *Black Elegies* is "where does the grief go?" And the answer is *everywhere*. It spills out of photographs and modulates music. It hovers in the tenor and tone of cinematic performances. It resides in the body like an inspired concept, waiting for its articulation. Grief is an ocean. It is an abyss. To quote Toni Morrison, it has no beginning, no end, *just circles and circles of sorrow.*[23] And the loss is tectonic, covering the surface of the earth while moving, shifting, sliding, and expanding. From sorrow songs, wood carvings, and deeply meditative spiritual sermons, to essays, photography, music, and film, black subjects have mourned what was lost even when not recognizable *as loss*. This book aims to highlight the center of gravity that is black grief. My intention is to spend time exploring the myriad ways black subjects attempt to live and mourn in and out of plain sight.

SIGHT

all breath travels out and up   disperses
and
cannot be followed.

—Vievee Francis

Ink and beeswax on paper conspire to envelop the viewer in a communal endeavor of palpable loss. Toby Sisson's *Black Tears* series engages the work of release in the production of mourning. Each tear is a 7" × 5" rupture in the linear history of black progress. They collectively represent the effort to encapsulate black grief into a legible text—that which provides a space of contemplation for the multiple losses sustained by black subjects over time. Sisson was compelled to create the artwork to address the extra-juridical killings of black subjects covered in the media, from Trayvon Martin to Mike Brown, Breonna Taylor, George Floyd, and Tyre Nichols. *Black Tears* is

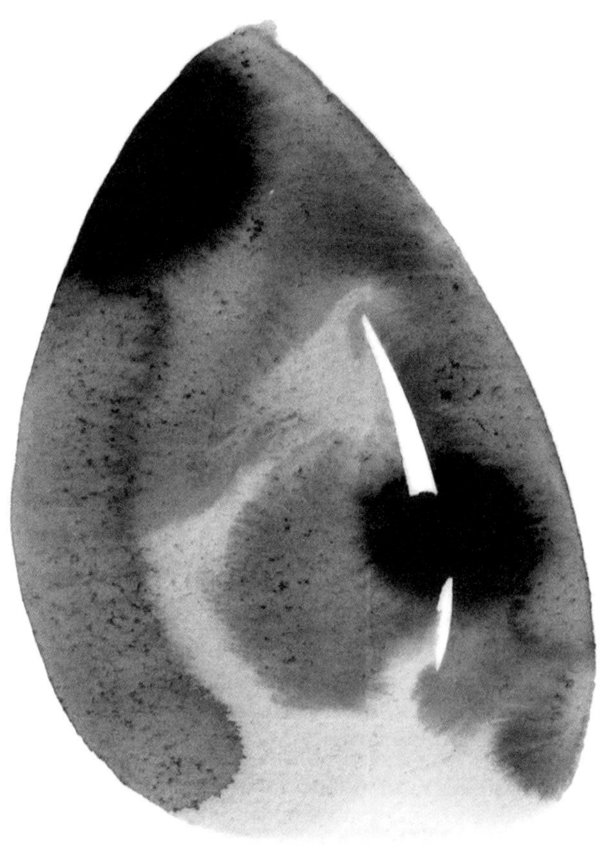

Figure 1.1
Toby Sisson, *Black Tears*, 2015.
Courtesy of the artist.

also an extension of Sisson's meditation on James Baldwin's book *Jimmy's Blues and Other Poems*. In this, she is drawing on a word/image interplay that Baldwin offered during his long career, one that privileges explorations of the burden of anti-blackness as it affects the lives of black people and black communities. Sisson is an abstract encaustic painter who typically works with large-scale constructions on canvas. *Black Tears* brings her concerns from abstraction to figuration in order to address black pain.

Black tears. In a letter sent to W. E. B. Du Bois in 1905, a graduate student at Clark University in Massachusetts queries, on behalf of his class, about the "subject of crying as an expression of emotions." Specifically, what the students really "desire to know" is "*whether the Negro sheds tears*."[1] This question engenders others: Do black people mourn their dead? Feel pain? Have emotions? The letter arrived two years after Du Bois's monumental book *The Souls of Black Folk* was published. In it, Du Bois went to great pains to illustrate what survival has cost black Americans. He opened each section of *Souls* with sorrow songs as epigraphs, to express how devastating the history of slavery in the United States has been for its victims, and how hard they have worked to manage the damage caused. As a visual experiment in cumulative trauma, Sisson's *Black Tears* grow and replicate—from a few dozen, to nearly one hundred, to over four hundred (and counting) individual and distinct tear drops that seek to reckon with the violence that often accompanies being black and alive. They represent black folks with souls, who exist and bear witness, who strive and mourn. Who shed tears.

Black Elegies is an opening onto the expansive artistic black world tasked with expressing collective grief while also grappling with terrors that continue unabated. I begin the first chapter of *Black Elegies* with Sisson's *Black Tears* to consider the intentional work of artistic production meant to tell us something about mourning, something about seeing. Tears are a multifaceted mechanism of release formed by the eyes and they assist in ensuring that oxygen and nutrients hydrate the surface of the eye. This clear liquid fills the eye until it overflows into tears that a group of white students in 1905 were unsure black people could shed. So we will *elegy* here, in this place of profound misrecognition until the matter of black lives is made visible.

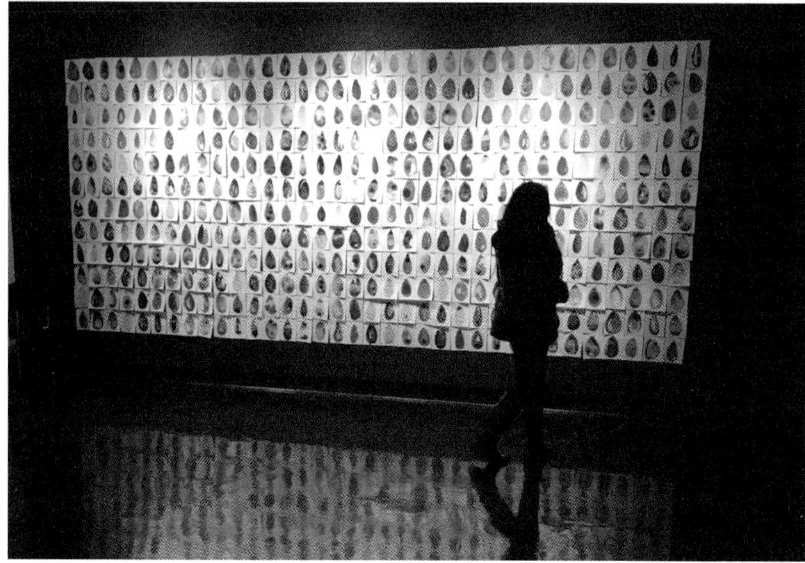

Figure 1.2
Toby Sisson, *Black Tears*, 2015.
Courtesy of the artist.

FOUR MEN

Four men stand in close proximity to one another, with varying degrees of visibility. Parts of faces are obscured, and what is not obscured holds the viewer in a space of sorrow and fury. Tina Campt writes in *Listening to Images*: "The choice to 'listen to' rather than simply 'look at' images is a conscious decision to challenge the equation of vision with knowledge by engaging photography through a sensory register that is critical to Black Atlantic cultural formations: sound."[2] Antiblackness has a shadow, and the demarcations of dispossession that augment its terrain are photographically contingent. For the moment I want to explore this contingency for the urgency and longevity it contains in Roy DeCarava's photograph *Four Men* and Toni Morrison's novel *Jazz*. The texts, taken together, are in conversation with expressions of grief both visible and invisible; expressions that flow like tears centered in a photographic print.

"A single exposure, a moment."[3] Outside a Harlem church Roy DeCarava photographs four black men emerging from a memorial service. The service is for the four girls killed in a church explosion in Birmingham, Alabama, in 1963. With this image, according to DeCarava, "there is a kind of movement . . . it is a movement forward, back, and then side to side."[4] With his poetic investments in the cadence and the rhythm of black visuality, the images he creates require more time to take in. *You have to listen to them*. Left lingering in the center of the frame is a face of concern and near-distraction. He seems to be elsewhere, perhaps trying to take in all the marked violence that a proximity to blackness engenders. Maybe in this moment he thinks of relatives, loved ones. Perhaps he is transfixed by a feeling of helplessness and continued vulnerability. There are tears welling in his eyes and they seem about to fall. He holds them, and the photograph is suspended in this space. A forever set of tears about to fall devoid of catharsis. In essence, this photograph, close-cropped and with duplicated tonalities, is grief in the frame.

Toni Morrison centers her sixth novel on this kind of "single exposure," this "moment" that DeCarava captures with his image. A photograph sits on a mantel, facilitating the process of mourning for a married couple, Joe and Violet Trace. This photograph is a tangible object of memory making and it is the image of a dead girl, who is not so in the photograph. Morrison describes the photo of Dorcas, the teenager loved and then murdered by Joe Trace, as one that was "not smiling, but alive at least and very bold."[5] In this, Morrison challenges Roland Barthes's assertion that a photograph is always already a "spectrum" of death. In *Camera Lucida*, Barthes writes: "because the word retains, through its root, a relative to spectacle and adds to it that rather terrible thing which is there in every photograph: the return of the dead."[6] Morrison's dead do not return as much as they remain, hovering between "alive . . . and very bold," in silent communication with the living.

Jazz is the story of the Great Black Migration, the journey in the late nineteenth century and early twentieth century from the rural South to the cities of the North. It is the sound of the wind that carried all those people and their dreams, desires, fears, and creative impulses, and held them together in something resembling a black melody—part sorrow song, part blues, part jazz and rock and roll. If African American cultural productions are practices in the sensorial, they ask us to participate in the endeavor, a dedicated acknowledgment of the resonance of sight and sound, the ever-deepening conversation that blackness opens out into the world. That conversation is filled with pain and its spontaneous release.

In Morrison's *Jazz*, Violet Trace attempts to mutilate the corpse of her teenage rival, traveling to Dorcas's funeral service to communicate with the once-living. It is Violet's repetitive obsessive insistence (she begins spontaneously visiting Alice Manfred, Dorcas's aunt) to understand her circumstance, and this leads to Violet "borrowing" the photograph of Dorcas in the first place. She puts it in the carefully ordered home where she lives with her husband, Joe. Morrison writes:

> Back up there on Lenox, in Violet and Joe Trace's apartment, the rooms are like the empty birdcages wrapped in cloth. And a dead girl's face has become a necessary thing for their nights. They each take turns to throw off the bedcovers, rise up from the sagging mattress and tiptoe over cold linoleum into the parlor to gaze at what seems like the only living presence in the house: the photograph of a bold, unsmiling girl staring from the mantelpiece. If the tiptoer is Joe Trace, driven by loneliness from his wife's side, then the face stares at him without hope or regret and it is the absence of accusation that wakes him from his sleep hungry for her company. No finger points. Her lips don't turn down in judgment. Her face is calm, generous and sweet. But if the tiptoer is Violet the photograph is not that at all. The girl's face looks greedy, haughty and very lazy. . . . It is the face of a

sneak who glides over to your sink to rinse the fork you have laid by her plate. An inward face—whatever it sees is its own self. You are there, it says, because I am looking at you.[7]

Dorcas's image, "the only living presence in the house," is both "calm, generous, and sweet," "greedy, haughty, and very lazy." In short, the image reflects the three-dimensional complexity involved in being human, and the contradictory alliances people experience mourning the death of another. In this manner, the photograph (and its attendant gaze) propel the narrative forward, through the couple whose mantel is occupied by the haptic, hypnotic, shape-shifting register of a dead teenage girl whose image says, "you are there . . . because I am looking at you." The multiple acts of looking and looking back organize the novel through the very process of improvisation that Morrison deploys. In this, Dorcas functions as the constant, allowing Violet and Joe (and eventually Dorcas's best friend Felice) to add their chords to Dorcas's. The song is different each time but utilizes a familiar refrain. And so, the novel shifts its directional point of view in order to emphasize the visual/choral/aural properties of black cultural production. The photograph is a centralizing motif of movement amid stasis, and allows us to grapple with loss, and its racialized disavowal.

If we think about *Jazz* as the elongation of photographic development, Dorcas comes fully into being only through an unspoken but collective ethics of care that the narrative mediates through each of the characters. This makes plausible the sustained attention to her memory (in sight, in sound) that keeps Dorcas in the space of the present. "Two or three times during the night, as they take turns to go look at the picture, one of them will say her name. Dorcas? Dorcas. The dark rooms grow darker: the parlor needs a struck match to see the face."[8]

Here's the thing about a darkroom or a *dark room*: the mechanics of the space necessitate time—to allow the iris to expand and let light enter the eye. And so Dorcas is developed in a time-released manner by the man who shot her to death and the woman who journeyed to her funeral in order to "see the girl and cut her dead face."[9] In this, the first chapter of *Black Elegies*, I am interested in the register of photography in *Jazz*, the construction of the elegy in jazz music, and the production of mourning that is highlighted by both. I am also interested in the back story to Dorcas's photograph. In her foreword to *Jazz*, Morrison says, "I had decided on the period, the narrative line, and the place long ago, after seeing a photograph of a pretty girl in a coffin, and reading the photographer's recollection of how she got there."[10] A photograph orients Morrison's writerly eye toward James Van Der Zee's 1978 *Harlem Book of the Dead*, and *Jazz* unfolds organically from there. The novel presents movement as the singular organizing force of black Americans, and provides a cartography of that movement that places music in communion with bodies. Our unnamed narrator tells us something important about Joe Trace and why he was considered thoughtful and charismatic by the women in the city: "they liked his voice. It had a pitch, a note they heard only when they visited stubborn old folks who would not budge from their front yards and overworked fields to come to the City."[11] Joe Trace sounds like home, and home in *Jazz* is a longing that has little to do with the temporal location of where people live or how they love. How loss looks or how it sounds. *A pitch, a note*.

ALABAMA

It is said that John Coltrane's 1963 song "Alabama" is structured to imitate the cadence of Martin Luther King Jr.'s eulogy, delivered on September 18 of that year, for the four girls murdered in the city of Birmingham, Alabama. "These children, unoffending, innocent, and beautiful," King begins, "were the victims of one of the most vicious and tragic crimes ever perpetrated against humanity."[12] Saxophone to bass, piano, and with Elvin Jones on drums, Coltrane offers us the sound of collective mourning. Mourning in plain sight, where violence meets a refusal of full citizenship while simultaneously engendering enclosures of black subjectivity. Jazz, the music, reconciles improvisation amid mournful wails with the possibility of resolution. "Alabama" depends on the subtleties of the unsaid, the sound of this recognition in an arc of collective emotion. Christina Sharpe writes, "In the midst of so much death and the fact of Black life as proximate to death, how do we attend to physical, social, and figurative death and also to the largeness that is Black life, Black life insisted from death?"[13] Coltrane might say that we must listen to it. "And so my friends, they did not die in vain," King continues in his eulogy. "They say to us that we must be concerned not merely about who murdered them, but about the system, the way of life, the philosophy which produced the murderers."[14] With "Alabama," it is not enough to simply grapple with loss, one must also commune with it, make a space at the table for grief, see it, touch it, and listen to its demands. Coltrane's elegy encompasses the negotiation of double consciousness that W. E. B. Du Bois presented as a particularly fraught black experience.

Four African American men visually negotiate the space of loss in a circular double consciousness that extends beyond the frame. If we stay here, though, we can hear the measure of Coltrane's subtle arrangement—the movement and the arc, the depth of his auditory field. "The seriality of the untimely forfeiture of black and brown lives . . . has become an urgent refrain that echoes backward and forward in time," Campt writes.[15] This refrain and its duplication demarcates the photographic space as one imbued with a poetics of loss that must be traversed carefully.

Musicians and dancers are prevalent in DeCarava's photographs from the 1950s and 1960s. He is seeking in that moment the thing they have in common with photography, how "in between that one-fifteenth of a second, there is a thickness."[16] This "thickness" is a visual demand on his part, and a measure of the absolute lushness of his images. This lushness exists whether the subject is clearly rendered and engaged with the photographer, is tangential to the framing of the photograph, or is an inanimate object. He is as drawn to architectural sites as he is to portraits of strangers in the street. Some of his images ask the viewer how much they believe it is their right to see, or they force an engagement that takes the power of a dark space as a photographic right. In Darby English's book *How to See a Work of Art in Total Darkness*, he laments the art world's "tendency to limit the significance of works assignable to black artists to what can be illuminated by reference to a work's purportedly racial character."[17] In the case of DeCarava, the photographer's lifelong attempt to render visible the aesthetic quality of his subjects was limited by a photographic history of racial containment, one unable to release black subjectivity from the framework of corporeal destruction. Using black-and-white photography but insisting on the more fluid range of gray, DeCarava's images emote a lyrical momentum, allowing the viewer to see the world how he sees it, from a darker tonal place. His is an artistic practice that says *I see you*, then *I hear you* in a photographic print.

When people speak of Roy DeCarava's photographs, they speak of tonalities, endless grays, fissures of content and form heavily dependent upon a unique aesthetic vision. One that does not fear gray matter, and one that isn't interested in the stark contrast of blacks and whites dominating photography during the second half of the twentieth century. He knows that most of us live in the gray zones, spaces less regulated, and under recognized. But what if we were to linger there . . .

Dorcas's image sits on the mantel in the Trace home, and allows the couple to mourn through the multimodal register of loss. Home. Family. Love. Need. The name, Trace, connotes the production of photographic memory. John Berger writes: "Unlike any other visual image, a photograph is not a rendering, an imitation, or an interpretation of its subject, but actually a trace of it."[18] Violet and Joe must "trace" the photograph back through time in order to move forward; they use Dorcas's image to do just that. Morrison produces in the construction of Dorcas's memory the inexplicable mystery of kinship that binds one person to another whether or not the ties that bind them are familial, intimate, or facilitated through the image of a stranger staring back with eyes that hold no expectation of the viewer or every expectation. This is the secret embedded in the photograph. Any photograph. It is a way of seeing that is here and not here. Past, present, future. The process of mourning for Violet and Joe, Alice Manfred, and Felice is atemporality of jazz. "He has double eyes," Felice says of Joe Trace. "Each one a different color. A sad one that lets you look inside him, and a clear one that looks inside you."[19] Though not visible, Violet has double eyes as well. Her only folly is that it took so long to allow the "sad one" to be seen by others.

The reader is allowed inside this space of collective mourning as well, since Morrison takes great pains to bridge the Great Black Migration with its attendant sorrows: separation from family, the violence of white supremacy, removal from the land. Is improvisation an attempt to both reclaim and transcend that land? Can it mark the visible in ways that allow for a reckoning with loss? Toward the end of the novel our unnamed narrator, observant, and seemingly everywhere and nowhere, offers a new description for the long-married Joe and Violet: "When I see them now they are not sepia, still, losing their edges to the light of a future afternoon. Caught midway between was and must be. For me they are real. Sharply in focus and clicking. I wonder," the narrator continues, "do they know they are the sound of snapping fingers under the sycamores lining the streets?"[20] In the "not sepia" "sound of snapping fingers under the sycamores" there is an acknowledgment of movement, landscape, rhythm, and the futurity of self-discovery, all of which takes place inside an enclosure of loss. *I see you . . .*

DeCarava imbues an intimacy of mourning with his photograph of the men, one that registers the extension of their concern beyond geography, age, gender, or class. The four men, then, do not occupy space left open by the murder of the four girls in Alabama. They instead supplement the politics of collective mourning to encircle and instruct. Here, in the auditory configuration of photographic stillness, DeCarava's pause is also a riff, an improvisation, and a coda. The photograph is a study in affect. The movement from left to right gives the viewer the opportunity to move across each face with intention, to think about proximity and refusal, and consider the costs of racial progress.

John Tagg writes: "There is a dark room. A shutter opens. The room is flooded with light that threatens to bleach the interior white."[21] Morrison's dark rooms are embodied relations, developed in close proximity to the tactile objects that facilitate memory making. They are both sight and sound, practices in the sensorial that resist a photographic death and instead opt for an auditory life. These elegies attempt to address the collective traumas black people experience while they grapple with citizenship so fraught that its very visibility is a problem. DeCarava cloaks this visibility in tonal proximity: photographer to subject, viewer to image. DeCarava's wish, encased in a circular refrain of black movement and the containment of space, is envisioned as an articulation of meaning brought about through deep looking and deep listening. Necessary for emotive release.

The drumbeat that closes out the first song from Ibeyi's sophomore album *Ash* pulls the listener into the heart pulse of the album's spiritual concerns. These concerns range from the deeply meditative to the resistant, to the haunting loop of repetition that signals emphasis. What we hear in the atmospheric release of the song "I Carried This for Years" pulls from the gravitas of loss to introduce us to something new in one minute and thirty-five seconds. The syntactical interplay—I . . . Carried . . . This . . . for Years . . .—supposes the listener is joined in the particularities of elongated grief, like a sorrow song that goes on forever. "I Carried" alters the usual conjugation of the verb "to carry" from present perfect to past participle. From "I have carried" to "I carried." It's subtle but visceral, like a series of teardrops on a wall with no end.

What you carry is both what is yours and what others have burdened unto you, regardless of intention. What might it cost to put our burdens down? And where?

"Years" is the temporal fixation that blackness will not cleanly abide. So the timeframe morphs into decades, quarter centuries, hundreds of years, and, potentially, eons. The load, then, that is carried becomes central to an understanding of who we are and why this matters. What you carry is both what is yours and what others have burdened unto you, regardless of intention. What might it cost to put our burdens down? And where?

"So a theme in your work is listening," DeCarava is asked in an interview by Ivor Miller. "Absolutely," DeCarava responded. "Seeing in the same way that one listens. To listen means to concentrate and focus on something that you are listening to. Seeing is the same thing. And waiting. Time is more important than all of that."[22] The photographer has stated that his artistic concern is with people: "What they do and what they feel and what they touch and what they leave behind."[23] Within the tremendous range of subject matter and the deeply meditative productive deployment of his photographic gestures we can see an artist intensely devoted to a particular way of seeing; to a particular manner and mode of photographic practice that does not dictate, but rather uses ambient light and sound to illuminate an already-present engagement.

Men, women, and children glide between the sky and the sea, disappearing into a space that is at once submerged and elemental. Jeannette Ehlers's mesmerizing video *Black Bullets* somberly commemorates the Haitian Revolution as the forward movement of people almost relinquished to history. Anonymous figures move across the screen slowly, effortlessly, as if assisted by only by air and ocean. They move from the left side of the frame through to the right, as they collapse into an atmospheric undertow that has the capacity to clear a path that allows something new to emerge. Filmed on location at the famous Citadel in Nord, Haiti, Ehlers, a Danish/Trinidadian artist working in multiple genres, turns her attention to the absented presence of the Haitian Revolution in diasporic memory. Faith Smith locates Haiti's "sovereign maneuvers" through a series of successful "emancipatory gestures" that

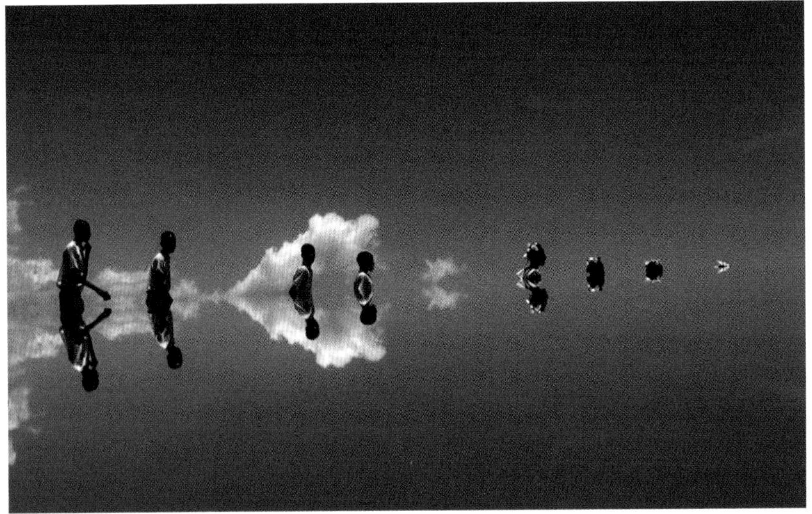

Figure 1.3
Jeannette Ehlers, *Black Bullets* (video still), 2012. © 2023 Jeannette Ehlers / Artists Rights Society (ARS), New York / VISDA.

produce "harsh retaliation" in order to stamp out resistance lest it lead to other calls for freedom.[24] Ehlers's subtle auditory dissonance works to illuminate the clash of history as a convergence point that Haiti represents. This convergence point is commemorated in acts of resistance that remind the black diaspora of its geographical navigation, so there is a way to mourn while continuing to breathe the air of autonomy. "I'm very much drawn to the body," Ehlers has said. "That's my material in a way. . . . I'm trying to produce monumental knowledge about our history and our presence."[25] Ehlers's collaborative sculpture *I Am Queen Mary* was created with La Vaughn Belle to represent the Danish relationship to slavery's legacy (Belle is from the U.S. Virgin Islands [formerly known as the Danish West Indies]. The two artists created the monument, the first to represent a black woman in Copenhagen. Ehlers and Belle, invested as they are in speaking back to history, make visible the sacrifices forced on black subjects who rarely get to imagine the other side of subjugation. *Black Bullets* retrieves the ethos of resistance as a slow-paced, somber, rhythmic glide into the liner notes of history. On the way each of the figures imprints the space with its individual and collective grace, inspired by the glory of freedom. "Black bullets" facilitate a weapon that, combined with speed and precision, can do immeasurable damage to the power structures aiming to refuse their sovereignty. Ehlers invokes the heaven and earth topography that merged in order to wade through water and envelope the sky. So that freedom could encompass the first black republic in the western hemisphere. As the stream of bodies dissipates collectively (in pairs and trios) or individually, the viewer is tasked with the work of witnessing, of commemorating, and of grieving. In its most elegiac formulation, it is the funereal processional that marks the bodies that the revolution has claimed on its way to free itself from the perpetual enslavement imagined by others. Here, Ehlers offers the repetition of revolution in a loop, or a circle. One that marks the visible with the glimmer of anonymity that casts the sky and the sea as libratory elements marking freedom as a thing "needful as air" and deserved by all.[26]

A voice reaches out from beyond the sonic accompaniment of bass, cello, and drums. Three words are released into the aural atmosphere: *I am free*. A statement. A command. A lament. A conjuring. A love story. I am free. Joined alongside Ehlers' film, the UK soul/funk/R&B ensemble Sault gives an offering with their 2022 gospel song "I Am Free."[27] The song opens Sault's *Untitled (God)* album and is meant as a route through the gravity of black life that must eventually lead to freedom as a state of release. Sault's mysterious emergence into the music scene is central to this ethos. A largely anonymous collective that began releasing music in 2019, Sault has almost a dozen albums to date. They range from protest songs to disco, funk, R&B, and gospel. With the ethereal "I Am Free," there is the replication of the slave spiritual, or sorrow song, with sparse lyrics, repetition, and modulation in the emphasis of the lyrics. How many ways can one declare their freedom? If *Black Bullets* is a sorrow song made visual, "I Am Free" is the sonic accompaniment that forms shape with each declarative utterance. Shape made form in the fleshy thickening of the arc and the reach of ecstatic freedom. And for the largely anonymous group of Haitians making freedom the centerpiece of their existence in the years beyond French colonization, the song beckons, calls, and responds. "I Am Free" takes a funereal undertow and drives it forward with speed that matches the very simple intention—to be free. It moves in tempo and pace with *Black Bullets*, as if it were its second soundtrack, and therefore merged with the film organically.[28]

Untitled (God) was released November 2022 as Sault's eleventh studio album. "I Am Free" is the opening track, thereby setting the tone for the rest of the album. Sault released five albums in 2022, exhibiting an eclectic range and remarkable depth of purpose and intention. If black love had a unifying musical sound, it would be Sault. *Untitled (God)* is meant as an offering to exalt the human spirit and take it to the nexus of illumination. Faith is love. Trust is love. Beauty is love. And yes, black is love. So Sault leans on those collective identities that tie, that bind, and invests in them sonically, so that something otherworldly can appear. Jeannette Ehlers's *Black Bullets* is the something otherworldly that appears as if out of the atmosphere. The figures emerge and disappear only to appear again. The work of revolution is slow, methodical work. It is vigilant. It is unyielding. The work of freedom never ends. It rages and wails, dreams and plans. It is an ellipsis that goes on for however long is necessary. Then pauses in the cavernous expectation of human will and infinite beauty. It waits in the shadows until you are ready to hear its call. It lingers, then trails off, knowing the signal it has left behind can be seen/heard by those in need. Like a sorrow song that moves from plantation to plantation seeking the listener attuned to the message in the call. I am. *I am free.*

Sisson's *Black Tears*, like Ehlers's *Black Bullets*, asks of the viewer that you take the time to contemplate the enormity of trauma sustained by black subjects on their way to getting free. For Sisson, there is this added detail: she is an associate professor at Clark University in Worcester, Massachusetts. The same university where Borgquist was a student when he sent his letter to Du Bois one hundred and twenty years earlier. I asked Sisson if she knew about the letter and her response was "I must have."[29]

BLACK MEMORY IN THE INTERIM

Soon after he arrives in Paris from the United States to put a measure of distance between himself and the country of his birth, James Baldwin is arrested along with a friend for the crime of stealing a bed sheet from a Parisian hotel. The arrest happens in the country that was to provide a kind of reprieve from the hypersurveillance, racism, homophobia, and criminalization Baldwin experienced in the United States. And so it is with a racially cognizant reading of his black presence that Baldwin marks the beginning of his decades-long negotiation of the self in public space.

After the publication of his first novel, *Go Tell It on the Mountain*, and his essay collection *Notes of a Native Son*, Baldwin becomes a notable figure in the literary arts. Importantly, his artistic gifts are put in the service of deconstructing the racial order of the West, since, as a black American living in Europe, he has unique views about the work of antiblackness enveloping the world. Director Raoul Peck writes, "I started reading James Baldwin when I was a fifteen-year-old boy in search of rational explanations for the contradictions I was confronting in my already nomadic life, which would take me from Haiti to Congo to France to Germany to the United States."[30] Peck describes the impetus behind his painfully beautiful 2016 documentary about Baldwin, *I Am Not Your Negro*. The relationship, violent and unyielding, between France and Peck's native country, Haiti, is partially understood by reading Baldwin. Threading together articulations of power and conceit is something James Baldwin's writings clarified for Peck. In the companion edition to the documentary, Peck continues: "What the four superpowers of the time did, in an unusually peaceful consensus, was shut down Haiti, the very first black republic, put it under strict economic and diplomatic embargo, and strangle it into poverty and irrelevance. And then they rewrote the whole story."[31] In this rewriting there are colonial powers with no dominion and imperial subjects with no past to recall or record. In the interim, though, black memory conjoins Peck and Baldwin in a discourse of the marginalized, and carries forth the language—literary and filmic, necessary for retrieval and repair.

To the photographic eye Baldwin is the quest. Presence, loss, recovery, intensity, purpose, joy, and longing—all can be found in any photographic representation of James Baldwin. Unlike other artists, both brooding and brazen, Baldwin's portraits seem less a construction of the man, and more an illumination of the force he was in the world. Part of this illumination is found in the simple visual display of Baldwin's impressive subjectivity. His sense of his existence in this world, and what the world required of him in order to remain.

"My father said," Baldwin writes in *The Devil Finds Work*, "during all the years that I lived with him, that I was the ugliest boy he had ever seen, and I had absolutely no reason to doubt him."[32] Baldwin finds this a damaging but not entirely unsurprising statement from his father. One encased within a paternity that did not belong to the man who raised him, but some other unknown man. He continues, "but it was not my father's hatred of *my* frog eyes which hurt me, this hatred proving, in time, to be rather more resounding than real: I have my mother's eyes." In this statement we have the symbol and the referent, the mechanism of photographic engagement that hovers somewhere between resistance and refusal. Because for Baldwin, "When my father called me ugly, he was not attacking me so much as he was attacking my mother. . . . I thought he must have been stricken blind . . . if he was unable to see that my mother was absolutely beyond any question the most beautiful woman in the world."[33] With subtle flashes of visual perception, Baldwin marks his gaze in the direction of the maternal force he has summoned through the ocular: "I have my mother's eyes." And it is with these "eyes" that he sees above and beyond the range of vision offered to most.

The masculine and the feminine, the mother and the father, the yin enveloping the yang. This is the photographic world offered to us by James Baldwin, through the portraits that represent him and the visual structure of the narratives he produced. If photography is the *studium* in Roland Barthes's universe, then James Baldwin is the *punctum*—he who punctures, wounds, illuminates, caresses. He who is both symbol and referent. "For the photograph is the advent of myself as other," Barthes writes in *Camera Lucida*: "a cunning dissociation of consciousness from identity." But Baldwin offers us no such dissociation. Baldwin's ocular narratology mirrors the image we have of the man. It is a probing, resilient, precise exchange of gestures, theories, and intentions. The epitome of ocular verve. And so I want to think of Baldwin as the photographic image-maker who almost never took his own photograph. I want to think of him the way I think of the very best writers we know—as a visual artist—an author who mastered the art of the eye, the side-eye, the look, the look back, and the clap back. For every possible manner and modality of the human face and its awesome capacities has a James Baldwin ready-to-go expression. For he wore the great range of his emotive extensions on his face, in his eyes, and through his gestures.

This is a matter of the visual. To attend to the world of the seen and the spectacularly unseen. In this world and its inhabitants, designations and demarcations mark the trajectories of movement and imbue them with meaning. Baldwin again in *The Devil Finds Work*: "The root of the white man's hatred is terror, a bottomless and nameless terror, which focuses on the black, surfacing, and concentrating on this dread figure, an entity which lives only in his mind."[34] Baldwin's pointed critiques, his unrelenting eye for detail and interrogation have entered the archive of his repeated and sustained humanistic endeavors. Because we have the spectacular production of Baldwin's engagement with the written word, it is possible the presence of Baldwin as visual interlocuter may need a bit of Baldwin's own radical attention to detail. For it is Baldwin's interaction with the world of the visual that most intrigues me, and tells me something about how he journeyed with grief in the frame of his visioning.

If we consider Baldwin within the expansive range of visuality and reckoning, his words carry over to discourses that negotiate the boundary marker of sight on sight. Between the religious rhetoric he frequently deployed and his deeply symbolic prose, Baldwin's structured gaze facilitates an order of the world that contains him but doesn't see him as he is. Baldwin's lifelong dedication to the honesty and integrity of his true form ensured a particular way of seeing, a way of orienting his eye to the interiority he had and always trusted within himself. His eye. In the text for "Remember This House," Baldwin writes:

The sky seemed to descend like a blanket.
And I couldn't say anything,
I couldn't cry;
I just remembered his face,
a bright, blunt, handsome face,
and his weariness, which he wore like his skin,
and the way he said *ro-aad* for road,
and his telling me how the tatters of clothes
from a lynched body hung,
flapping in the tree for days,
and how he had to pass that tree every day.
Medgar.
Gone.[35]

Baldwin's desire to be a catalyst of memory came at a cost to himself, particularly as he was scarcely given the time or the means to recover from each grievous loss, each death, every act of violence to which he was a witness or victim. If *where does the grief go* were a person, it would be James Baldwin.

From the moment he escaped the racist clutches of the United States to his multiple trips back, James Baldwin was a walking figure of mourning, rendered barefaced for all the world to see. It may seem to us now that he carried his grief well, and this is likely due to the constraints of time and the variations of movement allowed to take center stage. But from his first set of essays to his fiction and film criticism, Baldwin carried with him the full understanding of black life. A shadow figure stalking progress, antiblackness is the heavy load that Baldwin brings along with him everywhere he goes. Baldwin's 1963 book *The Fire Next Time* has its opening addressed, in epistolary form, to Baldwin's nephew and namesake James "on the one-hundredth anniversary of the Emancipation." As he writes to his namesake, so does Baldwin write into and through himself, as a kind of cudgel against total despair. "You were born where you were born," Baldwin writes. "And faced the future that you faced because you were black and for no other reason. The limits of your ambition were, thus, expected to be set forever."[36] Baldwin continues, "Wherever you have turned, James, in your short time on this earth, you have been told where you could go and what you could do."[37] Reflecting on his emergence as a child preacher at fourteen, Baldwin recognizes "I have never seen anything to equal the fire and excitement that sometimes, without warning, fill a church, causing the church, as Leadbelly and so many others have testified, to 'rock.'"[38] Ever cognizant of the power and force of sermons from the black church, Baldwin was able to incorporate his former life as a preacher into his writerly life.

The photograph of Baldwin holding an orphaned child in Durham, North Carolina, somehow renders with great potency the divergent and overlapping pathways of representation

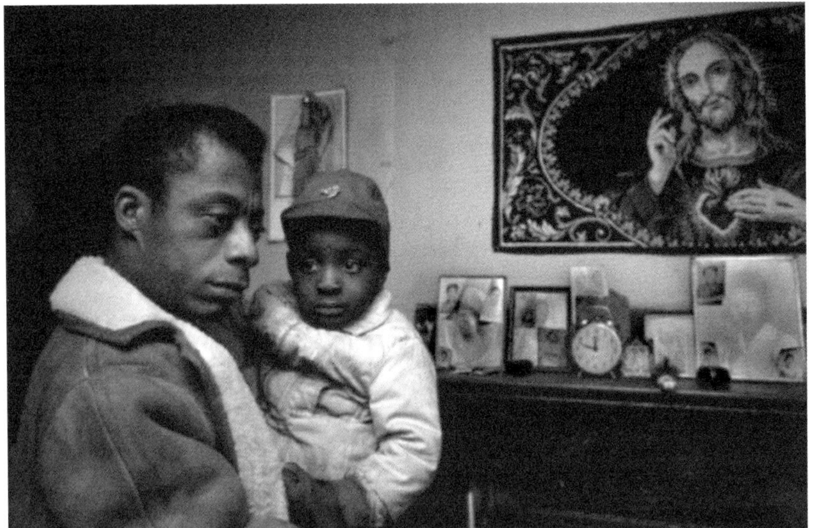

Figure 1.4
Steve Schapiro, James Baldwin holding an abandoned child in North Carolina, 1963. Courtesy of Getty Images.

that Baldwin's narratives evoke. Within the image there is the whitened figure of a biblical Jesus Christ, the symbolic register of Baldwin's past devotion beckoning from a slightly elevated place of spatial proximity. There are the dozen photographs lining the bureau in assorted frames, an ever-present symbol of loved ones who remain at once removed and a part of Baldwin's unique interiority. There is the child, abandoned, but momentarily held within Baldwin's arms, looking comfortable but cautious. And there is Baldwin himself, appearing pensive and slightly distant. He is not facing the camera.

As this image in its cropped form graces the original cover of Baldwin's 1963 masterpiece *The Fire Next Time*, it provides the viewer with another layer of Baldwin's photographic reach. Structured as a letter written from Baldwin to his nephew and namesake James, the coupling of this child with this writer work to extend the intimacy of the familial beyond the photographic frame. "Ultimately, Roland Barthes writes, "photography is subversive not when it frightens, repels, or even stigmatizes, but when it is pensive, when it thinks."[39] Baldwin's contemplative thinking in this image mirrors the thoughtful order of the gaze returned, so much so that the viewer is encouraged to think of the child as the personification of *The Fire Next Time*, since no image of an alternate Christ figure enters the frame, and Baldwin himself has refused the task.

An "abandoned child" is somehow the great subject of *The Fire Next Time*, always aware that there were other children nurtured, held, and loved, his very existence a reminder of all he has and will continue to see. And Baldwin in this photographic exchange highlights the shame of this without owning it outright. Because it is a shared shame, and every American citizen has to bear the markings of its structure. We can imagine James Baldwin in his multifaceted dimensionality: He is the cultural figure of the twentieth century: cosmopolitan, fluid, gifted, and rhetorically regenerating. He is the word and the flesh in the photographic imaginary. "When I was very young, and was dealing with my buddies in those wine- and urine-stained hallways," Baldwin writes in *The Fire Next Time*, "something in me wondered, *What will happen to all that beauty?*"[40]

All that beauty. "For black people, though I am aware that some of us, black and white, do not know it yet, are very beautiful."[41] Something of Baldwin's utilization of the photographic, knowing how photographs both highlight and obscure, is a reminder of the man in all of his full frontal insistence. If we take the iconography of James Baldwin as any indication, the writer is most prolific when he manages the mirrored constituencies of his artistic productions. He is, in his forceful yet relaxed photographic demeanor, the look, and the look away, the rhetoric and the reckoning, the symbol within the referent, and the eye on guard. *All that beauty* in one face within one gaze.[42]

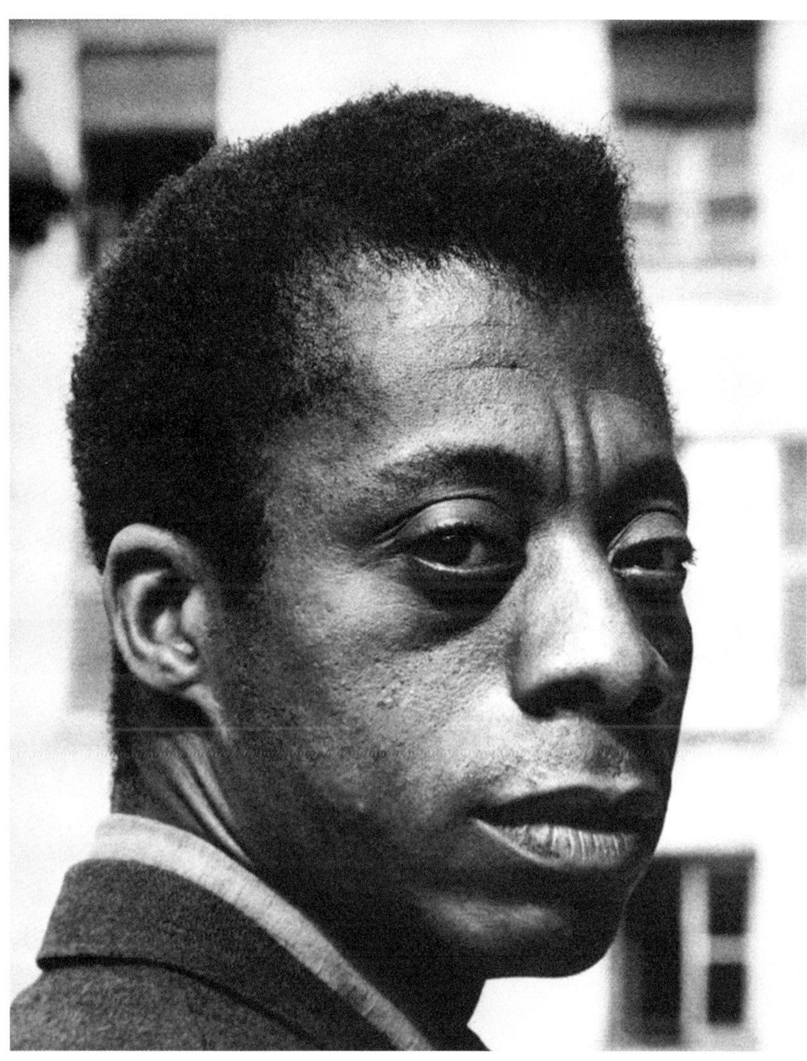

Figure 1.5
James Baldwin looks back. Courtesy of Getty Images.

He is a witness.

When I think about the modulations of grief located in black cultural productions beyond the genre of poetry, I think about James Baldwin's long durée into the vicissitudes of black grief. In every essay, fictional rendering, interview, and poetic inflection Baldwin endeavored to calculate the total cost of black survival within and beyond the nation state. In this work I contemplate sites of mourning that do not register immediately as archives of grief: the landscape of a gulf coast property, the interior of a vehicle driven by a former friend, a quilt constructed out of clothing worn by a loved one, a film to mark a country's reemergence after the defeat of slavery, a mural to mark the forced removal of a group of people. To these examples I add James Baldwin's unfinished book manuscript, "Remember This House," upon which Peck's documentary is based. I'm cognizant of Baldwin's elongated black memorial processes that, with aesthetic precision, encompassed multiple black diasporas under one worldview. In doing so, Baldwin's public persona serves as a central force with which to reckon, and this, of course, is bound by great loss.

Baldwin places three murdered black American men, Medgar Evers, Malcolm X, and Martin Luther King Jr. in conversation, "as a means of instructing the people whom they loved so much, who betrayed them, and for whom they gave their lives." Along the way, the film coheres around Baldwin's significant powers of observation, which he utilizes to lay claim to anger amid deep, racial grief. "That's when I saw the photograph," Baldwin writes of a walk in Paris. "Facing us, on every newspaper kiosk on that wide, tree-shaded boulevard, were photographs of fifteen-year-old Dorothy Counts being reviled and spat upon by the mob as she was making her way to school in Charlotte, North Carolina. There was unutterable pride, tension, and anguish in that girl's face as she approached the halls of learning, with history, jeering, at her back. It made me furious, it filled me with both hatred and pity, and it made me

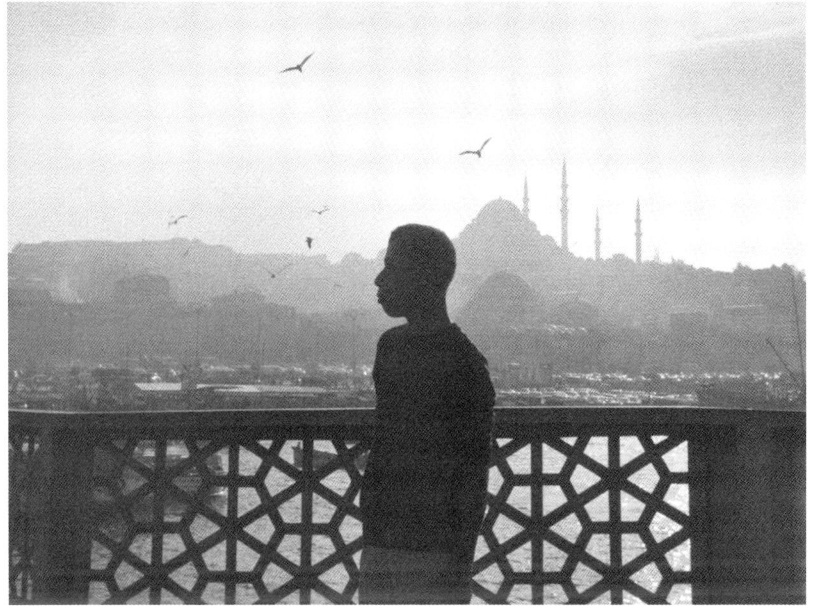

Figure 1.6
Sedat Pakay, Baldwin in Istanbul. Courtesy of Hudson Films.

ashamed. Some one of us should have been there with her!"[43] Understanding, as he does, the calculous of the collective in the face of racial terror, Baldwin wishes for proximity, for the intentional impetus of protection that numerical isolation does not allow.

For Baldwin, then, it was not just racial animus that compels him to speak, but the racial isolation that makes blackness its own kind of marker for others to further deepen an insistence upon violence. On "colorblind" racial policy in France, Trica Keaton writes, "Raceblind republicanism, justified in the name of equality, thus becomes a form of national gaslighting on matters of racism's production of race, and those who question the 'normalcy' become identified as the racists."[44]

In a telling interview from 1970 with Terence Dixon, for the short documentary film *Meeting the Man*, Dixon describes what he considers to be a recalcitrant Baldwin, refusing the directives offered, and ignoring suggestions the documentarian has made. What you find, in a twenty-seven-minute arc of increasingly agitated discourse, is Dixon's disregard for the writer he has come to interview. His questions, which sound more like accusations ("You do spend a lot of time between novels, why is that?"), are meant to diminish Baldwin's power as an artist and political figure. Instead, they illuminate the writer's stunning brilliance amid astounding grief.

This grief, as ever-present as it is resounding and palpable, is often illegible to others even when Baldwin goes to great pains to make clear the stakes of his humanity. After Baldwin answers the "time between novels" question, he adds, "I must point out, though, too, that I've been working the last few years between assassinations. . . . I mean, they're killing my friends, it's as simple as that. And have been all the years I've been alive." To this devastating admission that Baldwin has been "working the last few years between assassinations," Dixon moves with the speed of flat affect on the road to deflection. "Why don't you just want to get away somewhere and sit down and write your books? Why don't you want to do that?" "Because I am better than that," is Baldwin's response.

DIXON But you don't have to be better than that.

BALDWIN Oh, I do.

DIXON So you don't agree, then, I mean, when people say, "Oh, it's okay for him. He's escaped"?

BALDWIN What . . . have I . . . *escaped*?[45]

That Dixon struggles to grasp the gravity of "they're killing my friends. . . . And have been all the years I've been alive" is telling. He moves quickly on to the business of "escaping," perhaps hoping that Baldwin will allow this movement to stall the flow of his mournful considerations. He does not. But what if Dixon had been able to stay with Baldwin's directive, to pause as he had and allow the air to hold Baldwin's grief and rage in place? What if instead of Dixon's flat affect and quick dismissal we had an actual engagement with the writer's pain? What if Dixon could imagine that?

Baldwin's memorial production, the ebb and the flow of his gestural, expressive, contemplative visual display, is part and parcel of his engagement with the world of the visual. To encounter Baldwin's prose is to delve beneath the depths of human frailty and foreclosure. It is to consider the primacy of the visual as it orients the lives and labors of the citizens it refuses or holds close. To think of Baldwin, then, as the country's foremost theorist of race and the visual is to place him within the canon of interlocutors without whom we would have no contemporary discourse of visuality. His powers of observation were the enduring result of measured, potent analysis, cultivated over the course of many years, through several literary genres and in every imagistic presentation of the man.

If we consider Baldwin within the expansive range of visuality and reckoning, his words carry over to discourses that negotiate the boundary marker of sight (ocularity) and site (location). Baldwin's structured gaze in both documentaries facilitates an order of the world that must take his grief along with it. Baldwin's lifelong dedication to the honesty and integrity of his art making ensured a particular way of seeing, a way of orienting his direction to the interiority he had and always trusted within himself. His eye.

And Baldwin is most vocal about the loss that has shaped so much of his life as a writer, and as a black man. It is the loss of his country, though this is a loss he chose in order to save his own life. "In the years in Paris," Baldwin writes, "I had never been homesick for anything American . . . all of these things have passed out of me. . . . But . . . ," he continues, "I missed Harlem Sunday mornings. . . . I missed the music, I missed the style—that style possessed by no other people in the world.

I missed the way the dark eye closes, the way the dark eyes watch, and the way when a dark face opens, a light seems to go everywhere. I missed, in short, my connections, missed the life which had produced me and nourished me."[46] This longing takes on profound shape as Baldwin sutures his interiority to the black world-making that first made him a diasporic subject a long way from home.

GRIEF AND SURVIVAL

As a contemporary example of both grief and mourning impulses, and an elegy to those who have survived this, the protagonist in Toni Cade Bambara's short story "The Survivor" embodies a space of traumatic contradiction. Consumed by the severity of an abusive spouse and the memory of her fraught black urban existence, the protagonist Jewel's impending motherhood is a source of suppressed agony for her. In the story, the young actress is a repository of unwanted memories and although she is precious, as her name implies, she is unable to access the better parts, the jewels of herself. That which she is forced to remember renders her emotionally stifled, and these remembrances are at once vibrant and unrelenting. They include:

> Brother Billy on a dare leaping blindfold from a cliff in Morningside Park. The aged super, her friend over the checkerboard, being removed from the cellar on a dingy stretcher, starved to death, left to wait on the curb while the attendants grabbed a smoke and she shrieked, impotent. Carl Berry, who early, tenderly, gave her to herself, walking off the roof—the final high. *Great grandaddy* Spencer with emptied eyes strapped down under the rubber sheets as they turn him on like Frankenstein and she had signed and he had begged but she had signed.[47]

Feeling helpless and unable to escape the past or to process her own personal horrors, with "the mind off guard, an easy mark for all the one part dreams three fourths forgot," Jewel spends her days floating through time.[48] She manages the extremities of her personal and familial pain by drifting in and out of each painful memory she harbors in her psyche and gives birth to when her emotions demand it. Bambara tautly handles the impossibility of black survival, both self and other, without the assistance of the community to bring Jewel back from the brink of total destruction.

When the story begins, Jewel is on her way to visit her "grandmother," a woman who goes by many names. "And it was Miss Candy again, M'Dear, Other Mother as the young nieces and nephews called her, no one else."[49] For Jewel, Miss Candy is safety as well as torture, since Jewel is not in control of her memories and visiting Miss Candy has a way of triggering the buttons that lead to undesirable flashbacks: "Wives, she'd learned growing up in the dark, were the ladies found tied to scuttled boats at the bottom of the lake, their hair embraced by seaweed."[50] Jewel's interior battles, played out stylistically in the narrative by the unconscious memories placed in italics, guide the reader through the impending madness of the story's heroine. Emotionally bereft, physically exhausted and psychologically damaged, Jewel meanders through the narrative a tattered remnant of her former self, and yet only her subconscious mind attempts to understand why. Jewel continues, imagining,

> Husbands were men with their heads bashed in, doused with alcohol, stuck under the driver's wheel, and shoved over the cliff. . . . Wives were victims pushed beyond endurance, then snatched suddenly back from the edge by that final straw we carry from birth just in time to butcher beer bellies in the bedroom. Husbands were worms that turned on the *femmes fatales* who were too cocky to plot his death and got strangled with piano wire[51]

Jewel's tormented and abusive relationship with Paul, her lover and the director of the movies she stars in, takes center stage in the narration as Jewel attempts to wrap her mind around his demise in a car accident, her third-trimester pregnancy and the mental disease making itself present in her psyche. Theirs is a desperate, physical, and psychological enslavement, mimicking love, and their unborn child is at the center of their relational madness. During one of their many disagreements, Paul informs Jewel of his plans to move to a hotel room temporarily, and in return *"she found herself leaning on the breadknife, asking the arbiter below her ballooning breasts if she may take the giant step."*[52] Bambara creates in "The Survivor" a protagonist's journey that is impossible to navigate, as it bears down on the multisensory alignments of violences Jewel must endure. In the interim, the new life emerging seemingly has nowhere to go without absorbing everything that has come before it. "Black women's lived experiences," writes Juliet Hooker, "complicate how we think about agency."[53]

Paul's presence in the story is overwhelming, as Jewel refuses to see him in the past tense. She revisits moments of their frantic togetherness searching for images of her former self, the self which she no longer is. Throughout the story they elude her and she must settle instead for the half reality "coiled in her memory, springing at the last, seizing her at the casket and spinning her right around to hurl her into the collapsible chairs and up under the flowers, smothering."[54] The filmic display of Jewel's disintegration compels through the thickened narrative of imagistic bombardment. "There were ghosts in the kitchen," Jewell imagines. "She had stumbled aware of some night visitation that would reveal its purpose if she could wait."[55]

Although motherhood is not something that Jewel outwardly resists, the narrative casts a troubled shadow on Jewel's pregnancy, signaling a maternal resistance that emerges through flashes of slow madness. As Jewel travels to Miss Candy's on a bus, "she shifted her weight, not so much to balance the baby, as to juggle the mind's dangers, to ease the shouting in the head less it become a banging on the wall—let me go mad, Grandmother. Let me bleed and be forever lost and no-one."[56] Jewel desires a psychic purgatory where she can be no one instead of making someone. In her quest to slip into nonexistence, Jewel desires an escape that can ease her of this lifelong pain her impending motherhood would only extend. She embodies the complicated agony presented by cinematic representations of black womanhood. But Jewel is as unable to articulate her pain as she is to alleviate it. She journeys through her gestational torment as if she will be able to see her way through it in a fog, as if she will give birth to herself and not another being who will pull her further apart.

Miss Candy will be the midwife to Jewel's unborn child, guiding the young woman from embattled selfhood to disrupted motherhood. This is another kind of haunting, where reality is the "refrain that cuts to the core of the relationship between black feminism, precarity, and futurity," according to Tina Campt.[57] While Jewel is in labor, the final part her emotional stability takes leave and she drifts deeper and deeper into insanity. Drawing on her memories of Paul's direction and her screen acting, Jewel conflates her labor with a wrenching scene she must perform with her lover's help. The story ends tragically, as Jewel makes her descent into the world of fantasy and proves herself unfit for the motherhood she embodies. Following a succession of contractions,

> Jewel didn't let on that she was awake and spying. She watched the ancient dwarf pull the creature glistening with seaweed out of her left thigh. She watched them smile at the thing and then at her. The smile that meant if you didn't plan carefully, you would be destroyed. It was best to play the scene out with a few lines and bide her time.

Nurturing her dysfunctional relationship for years, dealing with the continuous decay of her community and immediate family, Jewel is a woman broken. Her physical and emotional breakages, slow, steady, and harrowing, are now her metaphorical offspring. Pain has been her only constant—the ever-deepening companion. The creative and inquisitive mind that once served as her artistic force has been transformed into a paranoid remnant of its previous self. "The Survivor" implied in the title of the short story is not Jewel, nor is it her soon-to-be-born child. What ultimately survives in the narrative is trauma-as-haunting—that which the reader is left to contemplate. She doesn't just see ghosts, she is one, and in this becoming it is impossible for others to rescue or recognize her. Thus, as a woman burdened and overburdened, raised by a surrogate mother, Jewel's journey comes to a debilitating close while she alone ponders the place of her baby, "the metallic monster in the mud encasing" that she feels she must destroy in order to free herself.

"The Survivor" asks the reader just how much black people—black women—can bear, how much they can create after trauma, and what is left after the trauma remains. In a series of narrative film clips moving from one space of fractured existence to another, Jewel is unable to see beyond her embodied stasis. And she finds it impossible to move on. So the story ends with a dissociative episode, where Jewel leans into her fractured psyche in order to make it to the next stage of her "survival."

Calida Rawles's 2019 painting *Radiating My Sovereignty* features a female figure floating in aquatic serenity, as water envelops the visual field. Both buoyed and gliding, Rawles imbues the image with a glistening ethereality that black subjects rarely receive in art or in life. The artist's large-scale realist-abstract creations provide the viewer with the unique opportunity to imagine blackness in its liquid configuration, with flashes of free-flowing movement accelerating the glow. These images glide as they flow, and signal release from the ties that bind one to the present or the past.

In Alvin Ailey's memorial to black women and mothers, *Cry*, a single dancer takes center stage for nearly twenty minutes dressed all in white. Originating in 1971, *Cry* was a birthday present for Ailey's mother with Judith Jamison in the starring role. It has survived as one of Ailey's more enduring choreographies, routinely performed to this day. As a ballet, it is known for the toll it takes on the performer of the dance. The difficulty

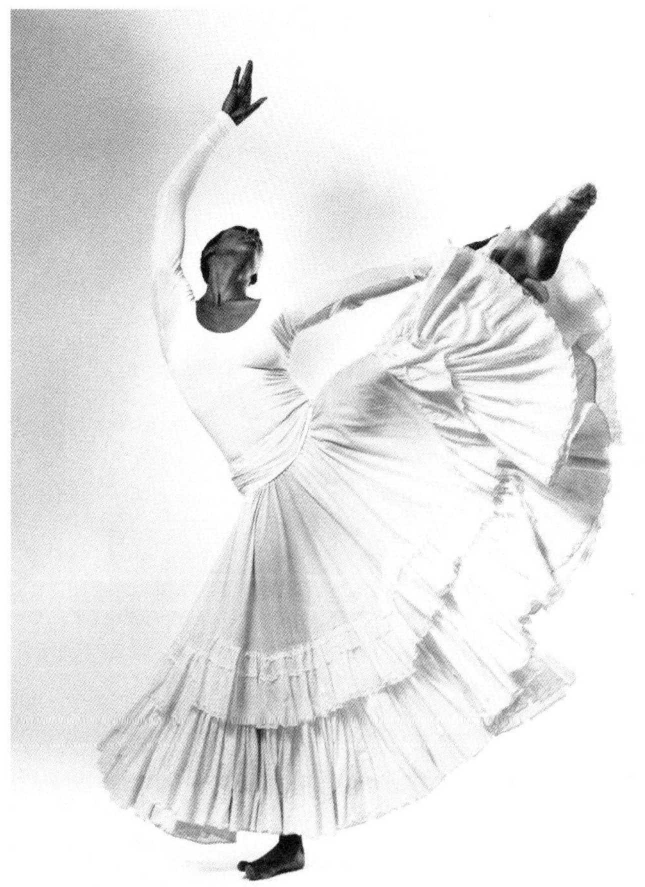

Figure 1.7
Judith Jamison, *Cry*. Jack Mitchell, courtesy of Getty Images.

of performing *Cry* is legendary, with dancers remarking on the bodily endurance necessary to complete the performance successfully. As an allegory of black women's tribulations in the country, *Cry* is a visual test of resilience even as it celebrates that resilience cloaked in mourning. For Jamison states, "Exactly where the woman is going through the ballet's three sections was never explained to me by Alvin. In my interpretation, she represented those women before her who came from the hardships of slavery, through the pain of losing loved ones, through overcoming extraordinary depressions and tribulations. Coming out of a world of pain and trouble, she has found her way—and triumphed."[58] More than this, *Cry* symbolizes an understanding of the relationship between embodiment and mournful release, particularly in the realm of triumphant survival. *Cry* was produced in a few weeks by Ailey, illustrating the force of intention the choreographer deployed. DeFrantz writes, "Cry ends with the dancer center stage, performing a full body dance of divination. Tearing at the earth and sky simultaneously, she moves in unabashed ecstasy, embellishing subtle variations in rhythmic accent with her hands, shoulders, and feet as the curtain falls."[59] *Cry*, as an expression of embodied grief, binds, contorts, and retreats in an effort to break free.

Lucille Clifton's poem *reply* provides an answer to the question posed by Alvin Borgquist so many decades earlier regarding "whether the Negro sheds tears." To this she responds, "he do / she do / they live / they love / they try / they tire / they flee / they fight / they bleed / they break / they moan / they mourn / they weep / they die / they do / they do / they do."[60]

We do.

2

SOUND

Perhaps the whole root of our trouble,
the human trouble, is that we will sacrifice
all the beauty of our lives . . .
in order to deny the fact of death,
which is the only fact we have.
—James Baldwin

We see a young man on the edge of an orange fishing boat, casual, playful, and carefree. We hear the sound of the ocean as his auditory accompaniment, and this feels correct. We watch as he moves with the ocean waves, sometimes rising to stand on the edge of the boat, sometimes toppling over into the water. When he falls, he does so playfully, rebounding quickly to return to the top of the vessel. He is long and lean, with sun-blessed dark brown skin. His hair is an auburn, blond, brown mix that tells you he is familiar with the warm outdoors. Ashes is a fisherman from Grenada, making his living on the

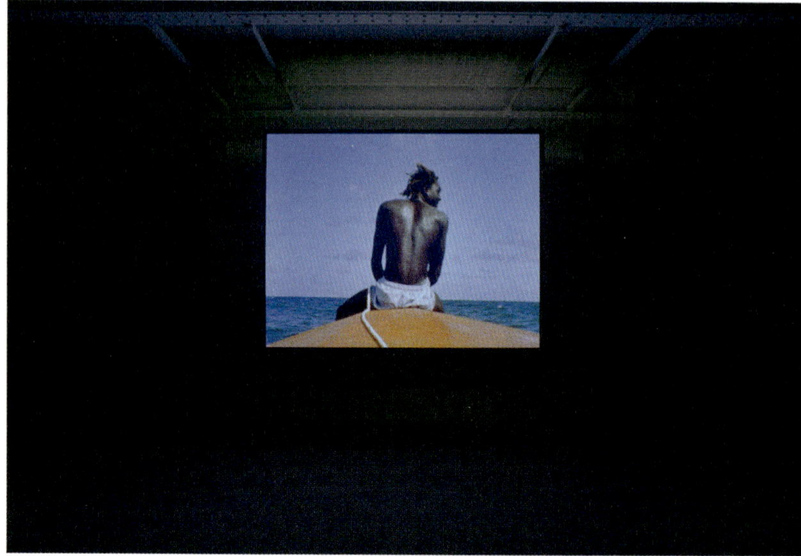

Figure 2.1
Steve McQueen, *Ashes*, 2002–2015. Two channel synchronized HD video transferred from 8mm and 16mm film, with audio, projected onto a two-sided screen, 20 min. 31 sec. Courtesy of the artist and Marian Goodman Gallery, New York, 2016. Photograph by Rebecca Fanuele.

water. He is twenty-five years old in the film. He will never be older than this. Steve McQueen's short film, *Ashes*, is a video installation showing footage on two sides of a freestanding screen that sways between two temporal spaces (2002/2015) in order to memorialize a life cut short.

Ashes finds a stash of drugs on the beach one day and he thinks his future is secure. The drug dealers track him down and he returns their drugs to them. He is then killed by the dealers. McQueen finds out about Ashes's murder years later and provides him with a burial plot and tomb. The second side of the video diptych takes place in the cemetery, where the tomb is constructed that will hold Ashes's remains. In the video, the young man's friends are in the process of that construction.

In what constitutes an accidental elegy, McQueen traveled to Grenada in 2002 with the intention of filming *Carib's Leap*, which chronicles the mass suicide event in the seventeenth century when forty Caribs leapt into the sea to escape French troops. While scouting locations for *Carib's Leap*, McQueen took a significant amount of B-roll, including images of Ashes in his comfortable surroundings. On grainy Super 8 film, we get to see Ashes in all of his youthful vitality. He is a compelling cinematic figure and he knows it. On the water or in it climbing his way back out, Ashes commands the viewer's attention. His laughter is our laughter, his joy our joy. We see him, then, in the full embodiment of the life he has before him. The film allows us to linger there, in the center of that life. Debuting at the 2015 Venice Biennale, *Ashes* traverses themes of movement, migration, colonization, haunted histories, and diasporic connection to underscore the intimacy between the viewer and the subject. It is a film steeped in the emotive extension of sound: waves crashing against the boat, the clanging of chisels against granite. The sound of goats and dogs in the distance. The narrative memory of a friend now gone. "Ashes is a good guy," his friend states in a voiceover from the film, "a brilliant guy on the ocean."[1] This charismatic, industrious adventurer brims with certain futurity in the film, as if his brilliance will forever be evident, forever be present. In its presentation at the ICA Boston in 2017, viewers were offered a still image poster from the film with Ashes sitting serenely on top of the boat, his back turned away from us, but not for long.

Accidental elegies abound in black culture, from Michael S. Harper's book *Dear John, Dear Coltrane*,[2] to Ryan Coogler's 2018 film *Black Panther*, where Chadwick Boseman's character is killed and resurrected on-screen, while Boseman performed this role knowing he was dying of terminal cancer, and that his off-screen death would be final.[3] The film, then, like Harper's collection of poetry, provides a lament for the dead who were still among the living but ended up encased in their artistic afterlives through the work of others.

My relationship to cinema is like this, frozen in time and also forward in time. Each moment I have been invested in cinema, it has been because the film reminds me of photography, retains something of its nature, its relationship with stillness. With *Ashes*, it is the opposite. Ashes, the still image, seems as though it is somehow moving, swaying back and forth with the rhythm of his body, and the rhythm of the ocean. If it were a song it might be a lullaby, softly intoning and imploring one to sleep. There is something soothing about the scene. Something that restores a sense of calm amidst a chaotic world. Sound animates emotion through memorial practices that focus on aural registers. Waves on a seashore, the recognition of the sound a beloved's voice from a distance, melodies retrieved after they have been forgotten, and even the sound of silence in a space of contemplation. This chapter moves between sight and sound to memorialize those moments of sonic retrieval, where grief is swaddled in the sound of release.

In Lucille Clifton's poem "blessing the boats," she writes:

may the tide
that is entering even now
the lip of our understanding
carry you out
beyond the face of fear
may you kiss
the wind then turn from it
certain that it will
love your back may you
open your eyes to water
water waving forever
and may you in your innocence
sail through this to that[4]

Ronald Reagan announced a military invasion of Grenada on October 25, 1983.[5] "This part of the story is history,"

Dionne Brand writes in *A Map to the Door of No Return*. "The coup took place, the Americans invaded. That was the end of the socialist path in Grenada and the English-speaking Caribbean."[6] McQueen's juxtaposition of Ashes in life and his resting place after death has the effect of sonically clashing, lullaby against a cacophony of movement, invasion, rupture, turmoil and afterlife. Black elegies are thus suffused with memorial traces that are geographical, historical, juridical, and cultural. This gives them a more expansive reach, and I am interested in the sonic arc of this visual production.

THESE (MOURNFUL) SHORES

For a site installation at the Clark Art Institute in Williamstown, Massachusetts, artist Jennie C. Jones creates *These (Mournful) Shores*, an aeolian harp extending the boundary of the granite wall overlooking a reflecting pool. Aeolian harp structures make impressive public art since so much depends on the capacity of the wind to provide an auditory assist. Jones's installation haunts the archive of the institute, whose holding strength is eighteenth- and nineteenth-century European art. Where, Jones seems to ask, does one go to ponder the relationship of the transatlantic slave trade within these walls? Where is the sound of the Middle Passage in this archive? A string instrument with origins in Africa, Asia, the Middle East, and Europe, the harp is one of the oldest musical instruments still in existence today. The extent of its reach as a global instrument is particularly compelling in Jones's hands. As the Clark Art Institute archive makes clear, there is an alternate conversation to have regarding western art history and European history, particularly when the traumatic events of the Atlantic slave trade are brought to bear on this archive.

With *These (Mournful) Shores*, sight and sound envelop the open air, offering a space of contemplation and redress for the enormity of loss accelerated through the Middle Passage. In the multiplicity of the "shores" in the title of the work, and the elongation of "mournful" therein, Jones sutures the

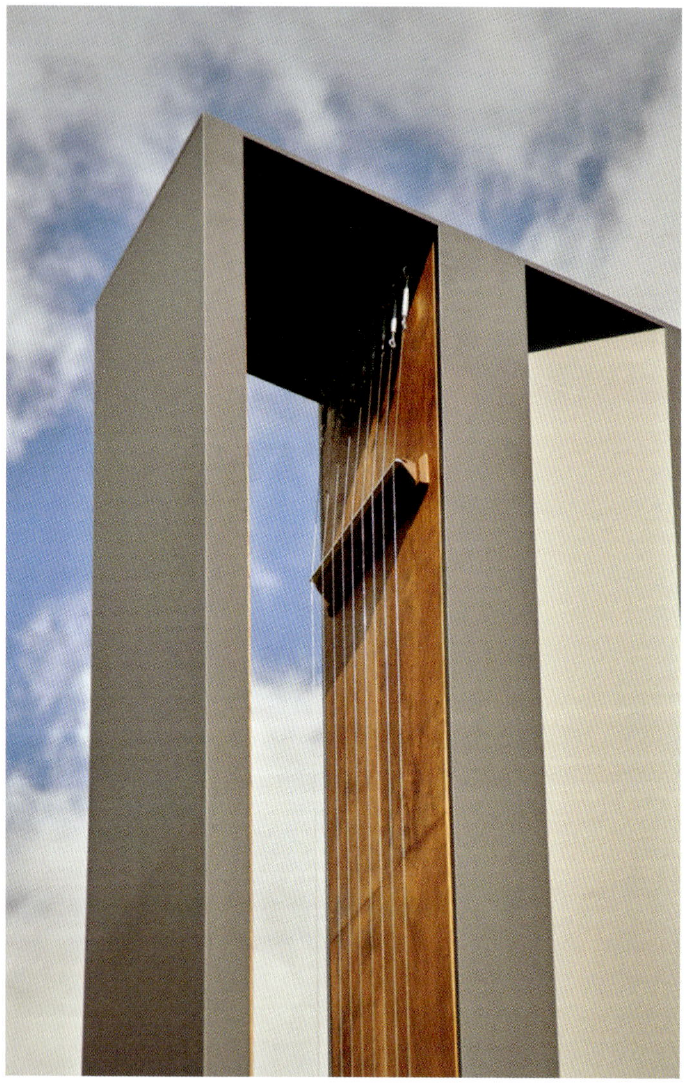

Figure 2.2
Jennie C. Jones, *These (Mournful) Shores*.
Courtesy of the artist.

violent occurrence of black Atlantic slavery with its archival dissonance, that which continues into the present with little resistance. An encounter with *These (Mournful) Shores* is an encounter with the ghosts of slavery, and the unresolved histories that are largely unknown to others. It is to wait for the sound of that engagement with history to summon you. It is to respond when one is called. "While it may seem an inherent contradiction in terms," Tina Campt writes in *Listening to Images*, "sound need not be heard to be perceived."[7] The spectacular achievement of *These (Mournful) Shores* is the time it requires for visitors to hear anything at all when they approach the structure. You step up to the harp, examine the wood and the strings. Step back from it in order to widen your view, and you listen. For what the wind has to say, what the earth has deemed vital, and the atmosphere does the rest. "Sound can be listened to," Campt continues, "and, in equally powerful ways, sound can be felt; it both touches and moves people."[8] *These (Mournful) Shores* is the boundless sonic saturation that places black grief at its center. It matters not whether visitors hear a sound that matches their expectations but rather whether the reservoir of trauma is able to silently "touch" and "move" people. And be present in its auditory absence.[9] "Black folk died in mournful collectives and in disconcerting circumstances," Karla FC Holloway writes. "We died in riots and rebellions, as victims of lynching, from executions, murders, police violence, suicides, and untreated or undertreated diseases. In such deaths, being black selected the victim into a macabre fraternity."[10] This fraternity, Jones seems to say, is not without its sonic register, its haptic presence.

In a conversation with Huey Copeland, Jones was asked about the relationship between abstraction in her work and the sonic. "I wish I had synesthesia, but I don't," Jones explains. "It's strange that these different musical and painterly references end up together in my work, because listening is so often separate for me . . . I often refer to sound works as re-compositions, so in that sense it like reinterpreting."[11]

Reinterpretations abound in *These (Mournful) Shores*, from references to European painterly traditions, to the haunting reverberations of slavery's earthly remains. Jones is attuned to these frequencies, be they sonic, visual, or atmospheric, as they inhabit space.

W. E. B. Du Bois is most attentive to the vicissitudes of black grief in chapter 11 of *The Souls of Black Folk*, a section titled "Of the Passing of the First-Born." Each previous section of *The Souls of Black Folk* seems to gesture toward the palpable space of mourning "Of the Passing" engenders. Here Du Bois is grieving the death of his first child, a son named Burghardt. The birth of his child fills him with a joy he could barely articulate fully. "And so we dreamed and loved and planned by fall and winter," Du Bois writes, "and the full flush of the long Southern spring, till the hot winds rolled from the fetid Gulf, till the roses shivered and the still stern sun quivered its awful light over the hills of Atlanta. And then one night the little feet pattered wearily to the wee white bed, and the tiny hands trembled; and a warm flushed face tossed on the pillow, and we knew baby was sick."[12] Burghardt Du Bois died of diphtheria at eighteen months old. On the publication of *The Souls of Black Folks* a few years after Burghardt's death, Du Bois's sadness and shock were joined by the profound responsibility of articulating the depth of his loss. And it follows the text like a cloud-shaped shadow of grief that trails Du Bois everywhere. Of his child's death, ten days after the onset of the illness, Du Bois writes, "No bitter meanness now shall sicken his baby heart till it die a living death, no taunt shall madden his happy boyhood."[13] Du Bois's only reprieve is knowing that Burghardt will not die of the thousand cuts of antiblackness blanketing the nation, where indifference and violence coalesce into something unspeakably inhumane but quintessentially American. "Black death and black dying have cut across and through decades and centuries," writes Karla FC Holloway, "as if neither one matters more than the incoherent, associative presence of the other."[14] By encasing

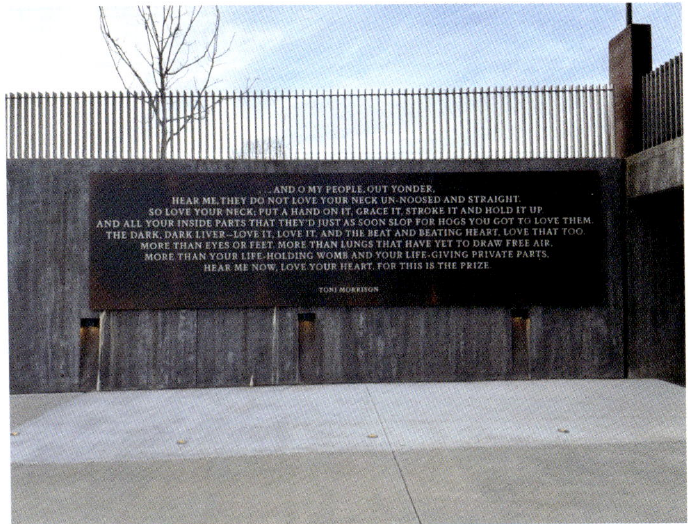

Figure 2.3
National Memorial for Peace and Justice, Montgomery, Alabama.

the fact of "black death and black dying" within his personal story, Du Bois allows his soul to commune with others who are similarly steeped in grief.

Du Bois structures the sonic life of *The Souls of Black Folk* through the sorrow songs that frame each section. Alexander Weheliye writes: "In the last chapter, Du Bois lists slave labor, spirituality, and musical production as the main donation of black subjects to U.S. culture and history, but still insists first and foremost on the sonic. . . . Not only does Du Bois project black music as the chief cultural nadir of the American nation, he also constructs—through and around the spirituals—an extended metaphor for black subjects' role in American culture at large."[15] I remain interested in the different sonic frequencies deployed by black subjects whose aim is to mourn losses large and small in ways that honor what was lost.

OF THEE I SING

In what is arguably one of the greatest renditions of the national anthem performed before a live audience, Whitney Houston (mezzo-soprano) emerges on-screen and offers the Super Bowl crowd in Tampa, Florida, her distinctive voice for just under three minutes. The year is 1991, and the United States is ten days into the Persian Gulf War. Race, sonic registers, and nationalism converge in this performance. It is unlike almost any other rendition then or since. And it has a referent. Houston said the only version of "The Star-Spangled Banner" she ever liked was Marvin Gaye's 1983 performance at the NBA Finals at the Forum in Los Angeles, California.

Dark blue suit and sunglasses—reflective—Gaye is accompanied by drum beat and keyboard. The previous day's rehearsal has many NBA executive types concerned. *What does he think he is doing?* "The mystery," I. Augustus Durham writes of Marvin Gaye's melancholic performances, "like the melody, still lingers on."[16] The performance is one-part gospel rendition, one part improvisation, and all R&B swagger and style. It's worth exploring what Houston found so compelling, so beautiful, that she used it as a guidepost for her own performance at the Super Bowl eight years later.

There is something bluesy in Gaye's rendition that Houston is eager to recapture, a kind of sonic high and low that mourns even as it celebrates and glimmers with the possibility of freedom. This, I believe, is why Houston and Gaye both extend the note on the word "free," signaling that this is work not yet done but work that must be done. Amiri Baraka writes that "it is impossible to say how old the blues is," and this atemporality haunts black musical performance. "It is native American music," Baraka continues. "Blues could not exist if the African captives had not become American captives."[17] Is it possible, in the improvisatory space between an elongated captivity and a relatively short freedom, to represent a desire not yet fulfilled? Robert Hayden's poem "Frederick Douglass" presents this conundrum of freedom as a temporal ellipsis, rather than a period.

When it is finally ours, this freedom, this liberty, this beautiful
and terrible thing, needful to man as air,
usable as earth; when it belongs at last to all,
when it is truly instinct, brain matter, diastole, systole,
reflex action; when it is finally won; when it is more
than the gaudy mumbo jumbo of politicians:
this man, this Douglass, this former slave, this Negro
beaten to his knees, exiled, visioning a world
where none is lonely, none hunted, alien,
this man, superb in love and logic, this man
shall be remembered. Oh, not with statues' rhetoric,
not with legends and poems and wreaths of bronze alone,
but with the lives grown out of his life, the lives
fleshing his dream of the beautiful, needful thing.[18]

With a repetition of "when," and "this," Hayden offers Douglass as a central figure of the nation in its pursuit of freedom and belonging. If there is no final destination for this "freedom" then all that Douglass fought for, his successes and failures, belong to the nation as well. Because if freedom is "needful to man as air/usable as earth," any refusal, national or cultural, is an investment in human erasure. It says the country traffics in images of inclusion that will never be fully incorporated, never real, and that this is the great irony of the United States. Its rhetoric of freedom is embedded in the reality of unfreedom.

What did Gaye know, when he sauntered, casually, to the stadium floor in his suit and aviator sunglasses, about what was to come? For him? For us? What did he sense in the moment, in the moments that followed, about redemption? Forgiveness. Mercy. Time. What did he carry on that day that we could and could not see? How can there be an elegy without clearly discernible loss? Marvin Gaye's stunning 1983 rendition of "The Star-Spangled Banner" in Los Angeles was filled with the somber undertones of grief. In its purest R&B

deliverance, Gaye's version recuperates Baldwin's "ironic tenacity" of sonic release.[19] To take the national anthem and loosen its war tones, replacing them with the singular voice of collective ecstasy, and all the while deceptively presenting the song as an upbeat groove meant to signal the collective vibration of those in need responding to the call that will get them home. "I want to walk down the street under the new trees in Detroit, and tell Marvin I understand," the poet Vievee Francis writes in "Marvin Gaye: Sugar." Francis continues, "To let his daddy go. / That—*trouble don't last* unless you hold on to it. / But that's not true. / Trouble is always. / He knew that. / You know that."[20] Francis marks Gaye's spectacular emergence into the archive of musical exceptionality that he embodied. Stalked by demons and by death, the soft voice meeting the softer face collides into a temporal abyss that failed to measure the possibility of his brilliance without also claiming the right to subsume him entirely. Marvin Gaye will die, murdered by his father a little over a year after this performance of the national anthem. His soulful plea during his NBA All-Star Game performance will follow him beyond death, and into the reservoir of meaning highlighted by his profound absence. Francis's poem "Marvin Gaye: Mercy" trails the avenue of meaning left in the inscrutable act that precipitated his end—that the man to whom Gaye owed his life and his name (Gaye is named after his father) would be the one to take that life from him. Francis writes:

> Take Marvin Gaye. His father had no mercy. Paranoia does that. Mercy is spat like spinach between the teeth. It slips out in a pee stream. Those without it lose it by adulthood. Flatline. It is replaced by a thin-lipped smile of rage. And with mercy goes empathy. But Marvin wanted mercy so badly from a man who didn't have it to give, as if all he once had now rested in Marvin. Who wouldn't be jealous? To see your better self. To hear all that beauty wafting out of every car window sweet as cigarette smoke. I don't trust those who don't like the smell. Orthodoxy. That was the gun in his daddy's hand. It said *don't* this and *don't* that and the

only goodness is to wither on your own vine. But how could a man in the flowering of his life, so much abundance, let it go? He needed. He lost. Lost to the one always praying who should have repented, whose sins (if there are sins) were all there to be seen as that bullet that set aside flesh. I imagine it differently. It soothes me to do so. Marvin spent in his father's arms after a cruel night. Envy replaced by pride in the son. His own wintry pride displaced by . . . love. See, even you can't stand such sentiment. So how much harder was it for Mr. Gaye on his high horse. Stomping down the seed.[21]

From "His father had no mercy," the speaker vessels through Gaye's personal familial conundrum as the center of gravity in a house of patriarchal refusal. "Who wouldn't be jealous?," Francis wrote. "To see your better self. To hear all that beauty wafting out of every car window sweet as cigarette smoke." And just as quickly as smoke wafting up and out of a room with many windows, the residue of the scent remains. The speaker reimagines the death scene "differently" from the known account. "It soothes me to do so." We are then offered an image of Gaye "spent in his father's arms after a cruel night. Envy replaced by pride in the son." If only a momentary reprieve, we take it. Because it allows for the temporary retrieval of this soft-voiced icon gone too soon and all too violently.

Marvin Gaye does something distinctive in this All-Star performance, so subtle and yet so very profound. You might miss it if you don't listen to the song multiple times. Gaye's musical performance of "The Star-Spangled Banner" takes Shana Redmond's definition of black anthems as its centerpiece. She writes, "Music is a participatory enterprise that requires certain performative knowledges in order for its political and movement aims to be realized."[22] While Gaye may not have been making an explicit political statement by performing this song in *this* way, he nonetheless understood the power that the combination of his voice and the national anthem would have on his intended audience. He was not wrong about this effect. I wonder, then, if attending to the visual apparatus of American flag imagery, while also listening to its sonic frequencies, can tell us something about the sight and the sound of a possible freedom, that which has yet to arrive? If we consider the ubiquity of the American flag, its mandates and motifs, the way it signifies on itself as a measure of the U.S. nation state, what might we uncover about blackness and its boundary markers? Gaye's rendition alters the lyric "O say does that star-spangled banner yet wave," to the hauntingly possessive "O say does *my* star-spangled banner yet wave." An intentional choice that references the way African Americans have existed on the margins of full citizenship.

Ross Gay's 2015 poem "A Small Needful Fact" extends Hayden's poetic concerns in his elegy for Frederick Douglass to that of Eric Garner, who is famous for very different reasons than Douglass.

Is that Eric Garner worked
for some time for the Parks and Rec.
Horticultural Department, which means,
perhaps, that with his very large hands,
perhaps, in all likelihood,
he put gently into the earth
some plants which, most likely,
some of them, in all likelihood,
continue to grow, continue
to do what such plants do, like house
and feed small and necessary creatures,
like being pleasant to touch and smell,
like converting sunlight
into food, like making it easier
for us to breathe.[23]

"A Small Needful Fact" begins: "Is that Eric Garner worked / for some time for the Parks and Rec. / Horticultural Department," and ends with the line "for us to breathe." Gay joins

Garner's life and his death with the natural environment that could not save him from an unnatural end. With the repetition of the adverb "perhaps" lingering between two lines, Gay allows Garner's stifled possibility to hang in the air like the breath taken from him in a filmed attack where a police officer choked him until he expired. With his short elegiac offering Gay links Garner's profession to the oxygen-dispersing plants that "in all likelihood, / continue to grow, continue / to do what such plants do" in a manner that befits the one (Garner) for whom there should have been an escape from external harm. Along with the repetition of "perhaps," there are the coordinating words that stitch together the hope that Garner's life intimated for the rest of us: "perhaps . . . some . . . continue . . ."

The relationship between blackness, grief, and what perhaps may continue is beautifully explored in Jesmyn Ward's 2011 novel *Salvage the Bones*. Esch, our fifteen-year-old protagonist, guides the reader through the odyssey of an impending storm approaching the gulf region: a hurricane named Katrina. Esch lives with her father and three brothers on ancestral land they refer to as "the Pit." The siblings are each steeped in mourning, having lost their mother years earlier when she died after giving birth to Esch's youngest brother Junior. The Pit stands as a forcefield against the coming storm, even as it has been slowly decimated from without over time. "My mama's mother, Mother Lizbeth and her daddy, Papa Joseph, originally owned all this land: around fifteen acres in all," Esch tells us.

> It was Papa Joseph nicknamed it all the Pit, Papa Joseph who let the white men he work with dig for clay that they used to lay the foundation for houses, let them excavate the side of a hill in a clearing near the back of the property where he used to plant corn for feed. Papa Joseph let them take all the dirt they wanted until their digging had created a cliff over a dry lake in the backyard, and the small stream that had run around and down the hill had diverted and pooled into

the dry lake, making it into a pond. . . . Mama, the only baby still living out of the eight that Mother Lizbeth had borne, died when having Junior.[24]

Amid this landscape of generational demise, Esch finds herself newly pregnant with no maternal reference point to help her navigate her impending motherhood. *Salvage the Bones* places nature and nurture in communion and in conflict as the Pit is presented as the neglected landscape that nevertheless provides some protection from the storm. Rooted in the security of this fragile home, even as the hurricane threatens displacement, Esch and her family navigate their collective interiority while their bodies exist mostly outdoors.

In this way, Esch and her brothers stand in solidarity with the land they know best, and the legacy from which they hail. They also listen for the soft undertones in each other. The whispers that say stop, rest, breathe, and watch out for grief. For it is grief that takes over the family like a storm with no sound, sneaking up on them in moments of peacefulness or disarray.

I am most interested in fissures of engagement where it seems a conversation about nationhood, race, and belonging is happening whether or not it is explicitly stated, offering a rendering or a reading not possible elsewhere. I'm eager to think through the meaning and the measure of "*my* star-spangled banner" as the group of people most frequently removed from its protective enclosure use the national anthem to lay claim to the country. Though this is not always a thing that registers cleanly, not always given the space the image or the song demands, it is a way through the scaffolded refusals performed by the state. And it is here, in a juxtaposition of race and nation, that new possible futures can be forged by sound.

I want to pause here, in the looping return of Marvin Gaye's spectacular NBA All-Star Game performance so that we can truly consider his offering. "The Star-Spangled Banner" is not usually the favored anthem for black Americans. That honor goes to "America," formally titled "My Country, 'Tis of Thee." The difference is minor but important. Instead of what is essentially a battle song of war (written by Francis Scott Key during the War of 1812), black Americans preferred the gentler patriotism of "My Country, 'Tis of Thee." It is perhaps more easily assimilated into the history of African Americans, perhaps more poignant, less bold, but I would argue that the evolution of "The Star-Spangled Banner," when black performers offer their talents to the song, is one way of envisioning the futurity of that which is beyond nation.

In 2010 the Carolina Chocolate Drops released their Grammy Award-winning album *Genuine Negro Jig*. The title track is a dreamy swaying instrumental piece that defies categorization. It is not properly located in one genre of musical production and it is not properly a jig: Hands, feet, fiddle, and bones. Those are the instruments involved in making this song. So much of the body is necessary for the cadence of "Snowden's Jig." It's heart pulse, mournful, joyous, subdued and ecstatic, organizes the circular motif of the song. Not a dirge, but not a jig either. "Fiddlers in the south," writes Matthew D. Morrison, "developed their idiosyncratic style performing for mostly black gatherings on plantations, or in segregated settings in parts of the country."[25] With the task of returning folk music to the black folk who created it, the Carolina Chocolate Drops endeavor to follow the example set by black musicians who performed with collective intention.

The band, then composed of Justin Robinson, Rhiannan Giddens, and Dom Flemons had placed the song in their repertoire when they were approached by Howard and Judith Sacks, authors of the book *Way Up North in Dixie: A Black Family's Claim to the Confederate Anthem*. The Sackses tell the band about the Snowdens, an African American family of musicians from rural Ohio, performing in the mid-nineteenth century. Their neighbor, Dan Emmett, is one of America's earliest white minstrel performers, made famous for one song in particular:

"Dixie." The eldest Snowden brothers, Ben and Lew, lived into the twentieth century (Emmett died in 1904). The Snowden brothers' gravestone reads, "Taught 'Dixie' to Dan Emmett." *Way Up North in Dixie* is the painstakingly researched story of the Snowdens and the circulation of their creative work. They composed and performed music and also traded songs with other musicians. It's clear that Emmett was able to copyright at least some of the Snowdens' music as his own, including "Dixie." I'm interested in the space between misapprehension and mimicry in a sonic/spatial realm. "Snowden's Jig" is the elegiac throughline that I want to offer in this book—a sonic reckoning that opens onto one possible resolution to the problem of race and its violent investments. One way to mourn what has been lost and what may not be recognizable as loss.

About slave spirituals, or sorrow songs, written and arranged by enslaved men and women on U.S. plantation sites, W.E.B. Du Bois wrote, "They that walked in darkness sang songs in the olden days—Sorrow Songs—for they were weary at heart."[26] To be black and "weary at heart" over racial violence is to exist in a vortex of visibility that has no resolution, offering the residue of black pain to an indifferent public. Grief, in its immediate and repetitive public presentation, is a burden that black subjects bear while the world watches, rarely intervening. I want to think about the enclosure of possibility engendered by a phenomenon Robert Burns Stepto refers to as a discourse of distrust. He writes,

> I . . . raise questions about the adequacies of the "social models" for reader-response literary analysis, especially since they do not seem to be, in Du Bois's terms, 'frank and fair' about the American "race rituals" that invariably affect American acts of reading. . . . In other words, storytelling narratives create "interpretive communities" in which authors, texts, and readers collectively assert that telling and hearing may be occasioned by written tales and the distinctions between telling and writing, on the one hand, and hearing and reading, on the other, are far more profound than they are

usually determined to be in those interpretive groupings constituted by other types of fictive narrative.[27]

Here Stepto is most interested in the space between fiction and storytelling that black writers negotiate with the understanding that misinterpretation and indifference will greet them. I want to extend this discourse into the sonic and the visual, so that we may explore the expansive range of black cultural production held within a circle of loss.

As with most arcs of investigation I find myself thinking about slavery's memory in contemporary articulations of grief. Black subjects have been in, but not of, the elegy as it currently operates via the literary canon. How then to figure the immensity of loss when the expression of mourning is curtailed? I'm trying to think about sites in the United States that harm in the absence of an acknowledgment of black pain. Specifically, I'm interested in the way plantation weddings highlight the incoherence of a producible black elegy. As Saidiya Hartman writes, "it's the place where the car hit the tree and your mother and brother died . . . but it's just a regular street for everyone else."[28] Except in this case this street is a space of celebration for others. A place where joy allows a particular demographic to dance on the literal graves of the people never meant to find peace. And so to lament the dead is a difficult endeavor when black subjects are presumed to be perpetually offered for use.

OAK ALLEY PLANTATION

A disembodied voice speaks in the first person, inviting visitors to Oak Alley Plantation, outside New Orleans, Louisiana. Located on the west bank of the Mississippi, Oak Alley is a former working sugarcane plantation dating back to the early nineteenth century. Known for the twenty-eight oak trees lining the pathway of the Greek Revival big house, Oak Alley makes for a scenic view, particularly if that view is absented of the enslaved labor force sustaining and extending its wealth and grandeur. Oak

Alley is tethered to a romantic view of the Antebellum South. Plantation tours usually minimize their own connection to the enslavement of African Americans, but Oak Alley's minimizing is nonexistent (they have reconstructed slave cabins that look like quaint guest houses and it has the largest gift store I have seen on a plantation tour). Slavery without slaves.

As a site of tourism devoid of the visuality of terror, the imagined subject is a consistent enclosure of whiteness folding in around itself. The Nottoway Plantation, located between Baton Rouge and New Orleans in Louisiana, is a 53,000-square-foot slave mansion that was completed in 1859. We might consider the normative structures that allow weddings to take place on slave plantations but leave no room for the participants to grapple with the weight of history when that history doesn't immediately bring these repetitive acts of violence to bear on the site. We could talk about haunting—both the ghosts of slavery and slavery's discursive afterlives. Are they able to be imagined as well? How is whiteness configured here as a commodity and client base? (In other words, who is duplicating wealth while also providing a spatial incentive for racial fantasies of hegemonic power?) If, as is claimed on many an online forum, people choose these wedding venues for the beauty and opulence of the space and *not* for the imagined enslavement of others, why are these weddings so white? (Also: "plantation" is always in the name of these venues.) How does the site change when black subjects enter the frame? What are the questions that can be asked/answered? What unknowable thing can be known? Maybe the task is for us to think deeply through this archive for what it can tell us about the history of slavery in the United States, the place of the Confederacy in our current national debates, and the continual refusal of full citizenship that black Americans experience in the land of their birth. If we were to stroll through these ruins, as Faith Smith directs us, where might we go?

Michelle Cliff's novel *No Telephone to Heaven* opens its first section with one word: *Ruinate*. This particularized Jamaican colloquialism is precisely what Cliff wants to privilege as she begins her novel with the merging of natural, national, and imperialist forces facilitating the cultural "ruination" of a people. As the novel opens, a group of revolutionary soldiers ("true soldiers, though no government had ordered them into battle") return to the rural part of the land to tame it and to take it back for the people brought to it by strangers. Distrustful of a built environment even if they are descended from those who built it, "they slept and ate outside, leaving the house to the bats and scorpions and lizards who now possessed it."[29] The ruin of the landscape will not allow the sounds of modernity and industrialization to rule; no plantation weddings with smiling white guests can be sustained in a space forged with the definite defensiveness of foliaged encroachment.

Cliff negotiates the import of the soldiers' linkages—land to body—as a tethering of generational purpose. Her protagonist in the novel, the light-skinned Clare Savage, embodies both the ascendant fluidity of her white ancestors (clarity), as well as the perceived barbarisms of those formerly possessed by them as slaves (savagery). As she returns to the ruin to claim it as her own (it is her grandmother's property), she marks the space of ruin as one that also buries its own history to create another in its place.[30] Hegemony, in all of its varied creativity is at the center of Cliff's literary concerns, and she uses the land as landscape, as the controlling and controlled feature of postcolonial identity. "Ruins may establish that there has been some break from the past," Smith writes, "and that something valuable should be preserved from that past."[31] Past, present, and possible future await the warriors headed toward their collective destiny in *No Telephone to Heaven*, and their bodies represent the shape this destiny will take.

Intending to supplant self-possession with a history of external ownership, land and body merge in the narrative as the group moves through the mountainside by truck. Modernity glides through the foliage of the past, bringing its inhabitants along for the ride. They journey up and through the landscape of their dispossession as the country they want to save, Jamaica, becomes more politically bereft, more invested in tourism than trade, and less resistant to appropriation by external forces. They are looking for renewal in the past. Resurrection in the land of the living.

Clare represents the embodiment of this absorption, and the hybridity of her lineage with its concomitant shame-inducing visual resonance is something she hopes to ameliorate with her participation in the group. Having "taken her place on this truck, alongside people who easily could have hated her," she hopes to use her grandmother's property as a gesture of collective struggle, the symbolic register of a tormented cultural identity, her own. The property thus tethers Clare to the ruins of the past, her compatriots, and their purposeful resistance. Cliff writes:

> It took the soldiers months to clear enough bush to have land enough to plant. At first they used machetes, fixing themselves in a line against the green, the incredibly alive green, swinging their blades in unison, sometimes singing songs they remembered from the grandmothers and grandfathers who had swung their own blades once in the canefields. Some passing the blades to their children, and grandchildren. The music made another human sound, combining with the human sound of metal against green, serving notice on the animals that the invaders were here to stay.[32]

Sonic conflation manages to merge laboring bodies across disparate historical moments, as the descendants of enslaved Africans perform the body rituals of slavery's remains "in unison" and cognizant of the "metal against green" that informs their surroundings. "We should recognize that our history is made up of different ruins," writes Giuliana Bruno. She shares Cliff's interest in the afterlife of empire, its movements and modulations, and the body landscapes it leaves behind.[33] The return of these descendants is supposed to signify upon the land what was lost and who has been lost, and this is a clashing of word and image that places black sound at the center. *No*

Telephone to Heaven endeavors to enact this demarcation as one that is encumbered by slavery's remains. And so the characters in the text glide between interior and exterior spaces, searching for a connection that might render their fragmentation less fractured. They are ambivalent about belonging since they remain compartmentalized and burdened with imposed multiplicities.[34] Comfort here inhabits the space of the ruin, where at least it is acknowledged that something significant, painful, and profound has taken place. The sonic features of these landscapes may whisper or they may wail, but in one way or another they endeavor to be heard.

"The archive of slavery rests upon a founding violence," Hartman writes in "Venus in Two Acts." She continues, "This violence determines, regulates, and organizes the kinds of statements that can be made about slavery and as well it creates subjects and objects of power."[35] Magnolia Plantation in Charleston, South Carolina, is one of the oldest plantations in the United States. Though it was a working rice-growing plantation, it is known for its gardens—the first public gardens in the United States—and the imagery reflects this. "By the 1690s South Carolina had codified the most violent denial of the enslaved's rights and legal standing," Lauret Savoy writes. "It soon became the only mainland colony with a Black majority, most on low-country rice plantations."[36] When visiting Magnolia Plantation and Gardens, what you are supposed to feel is enveloped in glorious nature and its ethereal qualities. Visually, the couples who have their weddings take place there do not need to consider the enslaved, since they would have no visual proximity to what this might look like, or how it might sound. Does the landscape have a sonic register that signals the devastation it has cloaked?

Or does a repetition of oak trees with Spanish moss offer visitors the splendor of the wedding event without the messy sight of the plantation fields or the plantation mansion? It probably depends on whom you ask.

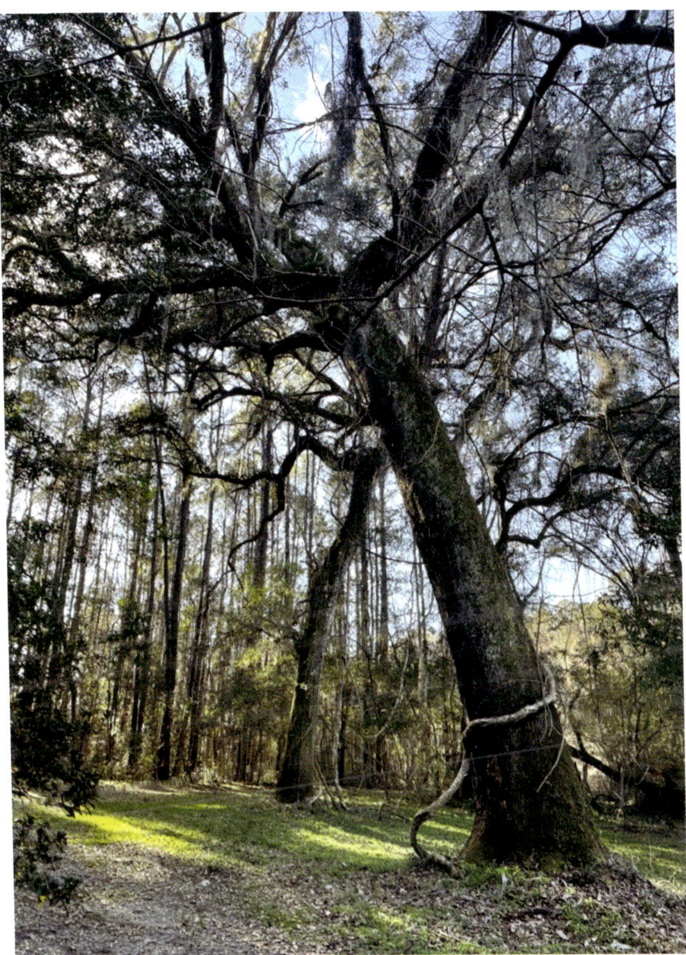

Figure 2.4
Enslaved cemetery, Magnolia Plantation, Charleston, South Carolina.

Elsewhere, I have written about this kind of visual dissonance, exemplified by Thomas Jefferson's beloved plantation Monticello, where the actual labor and trauma of slavery cannot be fully visualized. Instead, visitors to Monticello, where hundreds of men, women, and children labored with little reprieve, are treated to an accidental capitalist endeavor, one in which Jefferson was said to "loathe" to participate. Plantation mansions aesthetically display the violent architecture of slavery as a joyful white endeavor, one that can be revisited time and time again as a multigenerational site of desired reflection. Far from being a space of shame or revulsion, for these visitors the plantation is the pull—the promise of racial hierarchy rendered visible. I am interested in the disruption of architecture that corporeality affords. I wonder if attending to sonic encroachments on space can have a similar effect?

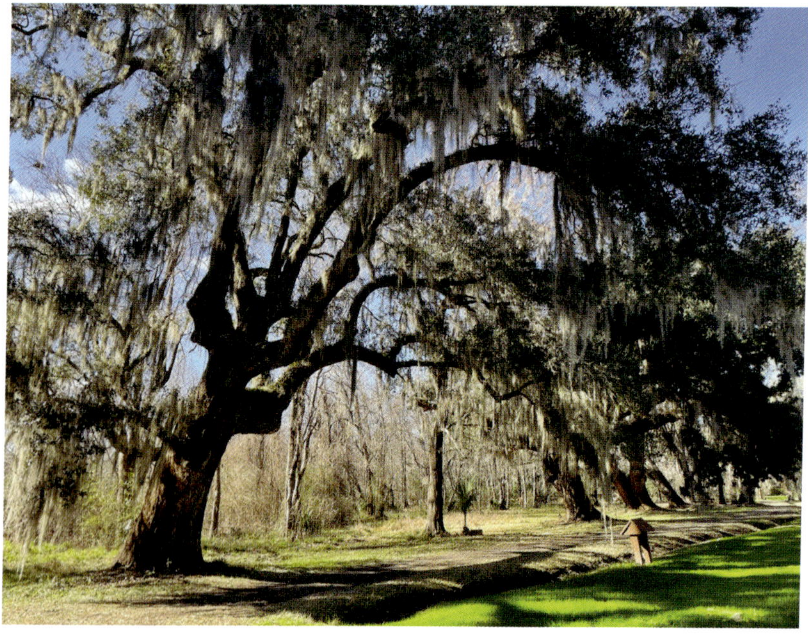

Figure 2.5
Magnolia Plantation, Charleston, South Carolina.

"Snowden's Jig" haunts like the figure Carrie Mae Weems embodies as she makes her way across Louisiana plantation sites in her 2003 series *The Louisiana Project*. The use of music to cloak grief is a way to refuse transience, to elongate a communion between the living and the dead. In an auditory keepsake, those who mourn and those who are mourned exist in space and time best able to resist co-opting by others. In my reading of "Snowden's Jig," Dan Emmett, like many of his minstrel-performing contemporaries, mimics without understanding what he hears. A jig. Where there is an expression of pain Thomas Jefferson notes what he imagines as its brevity. Its short life cycle. Of black subjects, Jefferson declared that "their griefs are transient" in his *Notes on the State of Virginia*.[37] Our contemporary refusal to redress slavery's devastation is a forward progression of this idea. That there has been no harm done. No people harmed in the during or the after of transatlantic slavery. This is the exceptional merit of Saidiya Hartman's *Lose Your Mother*. It bridges the space between the living and the dead, between grief and resistance, between home and elsewhere. "So much of black intramural life and social and political work," Christina Sharpe writes, "is redacted, made invisible to the present and future, subtended by plantation logics, detached optics, and brutal architectures."[38] A discourse of distrust regulates the parameters of black cultural production so that a malleable existence can come into being. I wonder about the places where slavery dwells in the imagination but not in its productive deployment. Places that whisper "slavery here, too" but scream white denial. A visuality of indifference that needs auditory unpacking. We are, perhaps, used to moving through so many spaces avoiding slavery's memory while reproducing its traumas. These monuments to slavery still stand. Some have been reconstructed and imagined anew, so that a contemporary generation is allowed to experience an immersive engagement with slavery's nostalgia. In the context of the United States there is a peculiar kind of dissonance surrounding this racial construction that contributes to the violence it metes out.

At the Whitney Plantation in Edgard, Louisiana, visitors participate in a materially embodied site-specific exploration of slavery. If "Snowden's Jig" had a spatial component it might look like the Whitney Plantation site, where an acknowledgment of slavery's human cost is central to the plantation's presentation. Visitors traverse the space that includes a granite memorial and database of names of enslaved people in Louisiana.

Inside the relocated Antioch Baptist Church, artist Woodrow Nash's representational sculptures of the children of the Whitney Plantation appear. Nowhere in the church can you turn

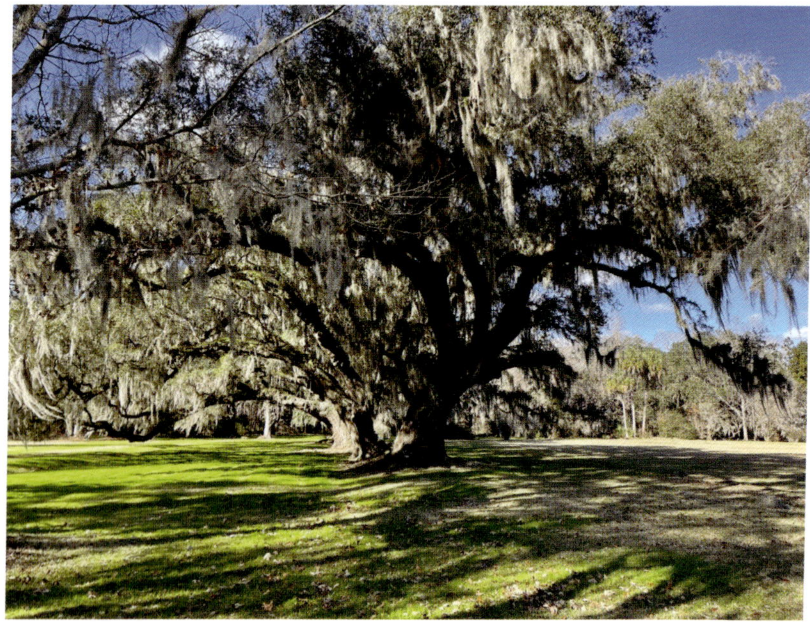

Figure 2.6
Magnolia Plantation, Charleston, South Carolina.

away from slavery. Every attempt will have a three-dimensional embodied reminder that the system spared no one. From the Whitney Plantation website: "Thirty-nine children died on this plantation from 1823 to 1863, only six reaching the age of five. The level of this death toll can be better understood when one thinks of a house where a child dies every year. Some of the children, either on this site or elsewhere, died in tragic circumstances such as drowning, epidemics, being burned or hit by lightning."[39] Though not without its problems the Whitney Plantation attempts to account for the living and the dead in a spatial formation that privileges the mechanisms of loss for those who have been lost. It is a quiet space, meant for intentional contemplation and redress.

You cannot hold a wedding in this space.

When W. E. B. Du Bois emphasized the highs and lows of sorrow songs as the entry point of *The Souls of Black Folk* he was imploring the reader to hear with the eye and see with the ear. "Sensations appear out of place as decay's beautiful disturbances," Ren Ellis Neyra writes. "A hypersensitive synesthetic reading method is open to 'vision' appearing in our fingertips or a smell carrying a sound," and this is how to voyage sensorially through black life.[40] Further, Ellis Neyra posits, "freedom is not the opposite of slavery; freedom horizons slavery."[41] Du Bois might agree.

LOSE YOUR MOTHER

We are immersed in the depths of grief, and utterly, wholly transformed after. Saidiya Hartman's *Lose Your Mother* reconstructs those stages of grief so that they include communion as well as release. Her guideposts are personal, archival, geographical, and methodological. She *moans*, along with the wailers, prays alongside the sinners and the redeemed. Like Morrison's *Jazz*, *Lose Your Mother* is an elegy with high notes and low undertones. And it exceeds the pace of its framework to reveal something new. Improvisatory and lucid, it reveals the wounds it understands as untreated. And it calls out the names of the dead. *Dorcas? Dorcas.* "It's the place where the car hit the tree and your mother and brother died," Hartman reminds us. "And your father survived but he becomes an alcoholic, so it's like he's dead too or worse. But it's just a regular street for everyone else."[42] Antiblackness paves the road that exists as "just a regular street for everyone else," ensuring that by land or by sea, the world is covering over the wounds of black folk, denying even the persistence of grief. *Where does the grief go?* Or in the words of Warsan Shire: "later that night/ I held an atlas in my lap / ran my fingers across the whole world / and whispered / where does it hurt? / it answered / everywhere / everywhere / everywhere."[43] Everywhere is the focal point of being black while grieving, and to do so in isolation, detached from community and kin, is to deepen the reservoir of devastation that drifts like flotsam from a nameless vessel. A ghost ship that peels off in moving increments to represent the dead. Hartman's movement from first- to third-person narration gives the book its sway, its movement from singular to collective, that encompasses the heart of the Middle Passage. A route traversed together-alone in the marked catastrophe of captivity. "But there were no corpses I could tend in Elmina," Hartman writes.

> There were no bodies draped in fine cloth, or rum poured down the throat of the dead, or dirges sung around the laid out figure. No one had sent a message announcing the death of slaves with a pot of palm wine, or fired shots to notify their neighbors, or tied their wrists with amulets and packets of gold dust for the journey to the next world. No one did these things for them, or fasted, or held a wake for two nights with drumming and dancing. No one placed burial gifts alongside the corpse or whispered messages that were to be delivered to dead relatives in the land of ghosts.[44]

In the sonic resonance of *no one* is the atmospheric divide, corporally rendered. All those bodies passing through a space necessarily alter its components, its rifts and tide. Unnamed though they may be, the energy released into the earth will still exist. One, after another, and another will be counted, with or without names. "I am the name of the sound and the sound of the name," the epigraph to *Jazz* reminds us.[45] Hartman's concerns culminate in chapter 7 of *Lose Your Mother*, a section called "The Dead Book." Here, she outlines the failed repetitions on a slave vessel named *Recovery*, where a captive girl was murdered on a ship and "not even her name survived."[46] Understanding that fragments of the girl's story do not constitute a whole, Hartman nonetheless offers us a way to read her into the archive of black grief. "Looking at the Atlantic," Hartman laments, "I thought of the girl."[47] Conjuring all of the possibilities for retrieval, Hartman engages in an extension of her theorized "critical fabulation" in order to bring into existence more than just "a few lines from a musty trial transcript" that constitute "the entire story of the girl's life."[48] Instead, Hartman's elegiac disruption offers the mourner multiple opportunities to participate in the girl's temporary resurrection, her collective reprieve. To bring her back from the dead, even temporarily, is to pull at the seams of the transatlantic slave trade, its routes and rhetorical dimensions, to unravel its violent gestural illogic. The girl killed on the *Recovery* is not the only one among its dead, but in using her story as a focal point of "The Dead Book," Hartman is asking us not to avert our gaze this time, and to attend to the patterns of memorial conjuring that give way to the strictures of the historical record we have yet to fully grapple with.

IN SIGHT, IN SOUND

In Amanda Russhell Wallace's 2011 short film *Mo(u)rning Tea, Extracted*, the artist creates a meditation on black women's grief using the solitary reference point of her own body, alongside lines of verse from Octavia Butler's novel *Kindred* and Gayl Jones's *Corregidora*. *Kindred* is placed alongside *Corregidora* so that Wallace's artistic investments are most closely aligned with the memory of slavery as it impacts and imperils black women in the present. Under the performed mechanics of setting up and preparing tea within a domestic space, Wallace enacts a sight/sound dialectic in order to mourn those who have passed. Instead of presenting herself as a widow mourning the loss of her husband, Wallace instead represents the loss (and subsequent grieving) of black women's acknowledged history under slavery as a layer of subterfuge that she must unpack with the practice of her deliberate embodiment. The artist is tethered to a corridor/hallway that splits the scene from the exteriority of the veiled figure in black, walking back and forth through the interior space, and the interiority of another figure, also played by Wallace. Nearly silhouetted against light and shadow as a voice-over lays out the parameters of loss and mourning stalking black female subjectivities, Wallace communes with the atmospheric enclosure of loss.[49] The figure steps in and out of the frame as a haunting, gesturing toward the environment of grief that orients the film. Michael Boyce Gillespie writes, "The vast modalities of black art, of which cinema is a part, often suffer the analytic impropriety of marginality, selective blindness, and indifference to the discursivity of race and blackness as potentiality."[50] *Mo(u)rning Tea, Extracted* utilizes "blackness as potentiality" within a black feminist framework that centers a process of grieving within the interiority of the architecture of careful enclosures, those that allow the transmission of the sight and sound of mourning to fill interior space.

And thus, the two figures occupy the domicile at different moments, in light, and in shadow: one to articulate the lower frequencies of all that has been taken or lost, and the other to contextualize this loss as a series of movements in and out of the frame. Wallace imbues the domestic sphere with a slow, methodical rhythm and flow, the contours of which haunt the discourse of slavery in the United States and its afterlives. Each step is a gesture, toward the *could-have-been* that occupies slavery's memory in an ambulatory refrain that encircles itself. The pace of the film is a modulation—parts of a whole—in communion with the present past of black dispossession.

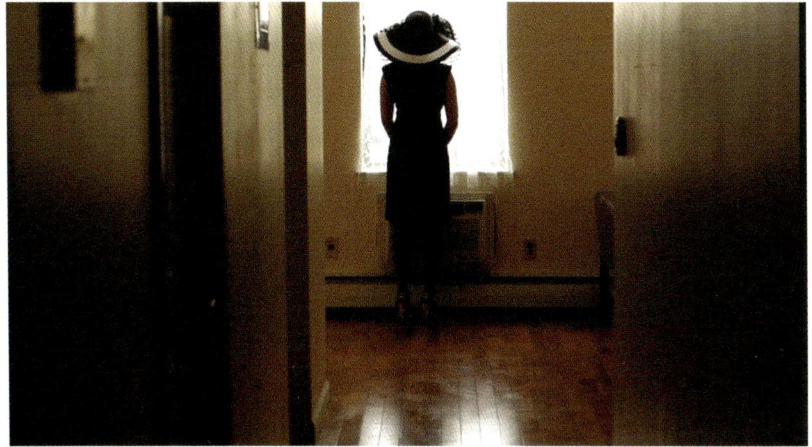

Figure 2.7
Amanda Russhell Wallace, *Mo(u)rning Tea, Extracted*, 2011.

BLACK MARY

It's thirteen seconds before you see Alice Smith in Kahlil Joseph's short film *Black Mary*. You hear her voice two seconds before you see her. It's haunting, this entrance in the film by Smith, who is singer, spirit, and muse. *Black Mary*, commissioned by the Tate Museum, is an ode to the photographic oeuvre of Roy DeCarava and merges sound with deeply saturated images of black subjectivity. Smith is the focal point; she is the center of the text. It is her voice you follow. It is her world you enter. She sings a rendition of "I Put a Spell on You" and you are spellbound. The tone of the song betrays its lyrics. Or maybe it doesn't. Made famous first by Screamin' Jay Hawkins and Nina Simone, Smith's remake is unlike any other that exists. It possesses all of the soul and the edge of other performances but is cognizant of the plead, the tortured possessive quest. The song winds like a road, curved and smooth, but devoid of destination. Blackness *is* the destination and the mood is full of collective grief. It is an insistent wail that goes on for six and a half minutes. The tempo is slowed as Smith's four-octave vocal range glides in and out. A haunting. A love story. A prayer. A wail. An elegy. She is sparing with the lyrics, repeating words like "mine" and "I love you" until they are disaggregated from the form they once held and returned to their place of origin. Joseph's use of Smith as the focal point in *Black Mary* is explained in this quote from a conversation the artist had with Arthur Jafa: "I have a pure obsession with Alice Smith. A lot of people do. When she sings, especially live, she goes places very few people I've ever seen can create . . . there's a lot of pain and soul in her songs . . . it's formed by everything (that's happened in the last 400 years or so) . . . a kind of cry, it feels like a cry."[51] To represent 400 years of pain, in a voice that sounds like a cry, is to expand the framework of mourning so that it represents "the living and the dead," to quote Toni Morrison. The slow-moving mix of imagery is punctuated by sound and anchored by Smith's voice. Hilton Als writes of Kahlil Joseph, "A master of sound, he allows the dialogue and the music in his movies to drop out and then return at unexpected moments, creating a sometimes heart-stopping juxtaposition between what we hear and what we see. It's as if Joseph's visual world were a vinyl record, complete with scratches that make the needle skip, thereby changing the flow of things."[52] Joseph's attentiveness to the vicissitudes of grief is evident in all his films, which have a mellow haunting quality to them. *Black Mary* is an engagement with our very present moment of blackness, of sight, of sound, and of mourning. Joseph has said that the title is to represent "Black Mary" as a protective force against police violence. From the enclosure of interior space Smith sings while swaying back and forth, captured repeatedly alone or among others. Joseph's gaze lingers long and lovingly over the subjects in the film, guided by Smith's musical performance. As quiet as it is thunderous, the mourning properties of *Black Mary* hover and drift; they are on streets, inside homes, and on the faces of black subjects Joseph wants you to see. To hear. To touch.

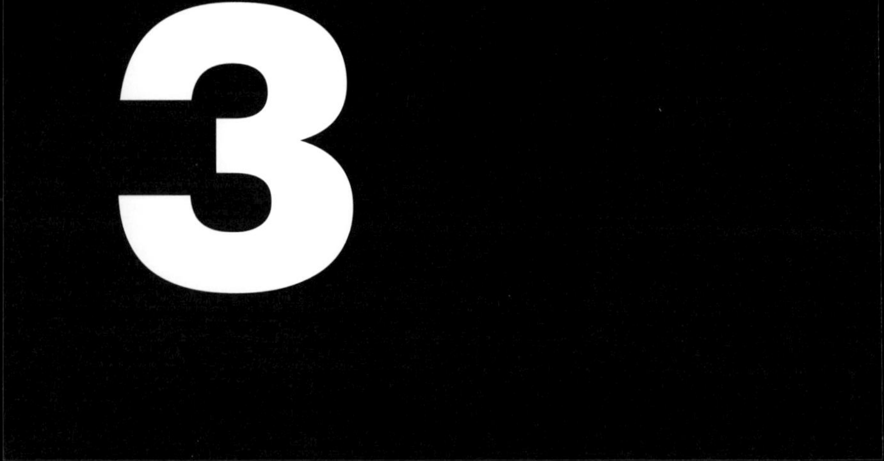
3

TOUCH

It was your tenderness—
a tenderness so delicate
I thought it could not last,
but last it did and envelop me it did.
—Toni Morrison

The final section of Barry Jenkins's 2016 film *Moonlight* is an addition that does not exist in Tarell Alvin McCraney's play *In Moonlight Black Boys Look Blue*. In an interview Jenkins states: "The endpoint of the film is not the end point of the original piece. [McCraney] stopped writing at the point where Chiron is making the decision to drive back to Miami to see Kevin. So I kept going."[1] This decision to "keep going" offers the viewer not just a temporal extension of Kevin and Chiron's story, but also an expansively resplendent coupling of haptic regard. Looks that touch, heighten, hold, anticipate, and linger. From the initial shot of Chiron, or Black, as he is known

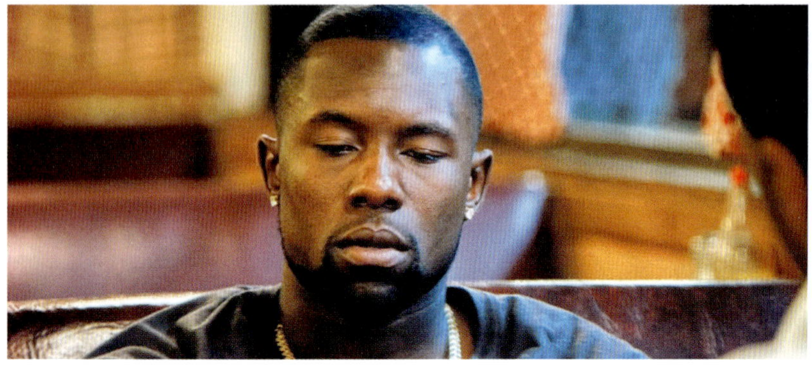

Figure 3.1
Barry Jenkins, dir., *Moonlight*, A24 / Plan B Entertainment, 2016.

(played by Trevante Rhodes) driving with patient purpose in the direction of Kevin (played by André Holland), to the closing scene with the two men tenderly enveloped, Chiron's head gently placed on Kevin's shoulder, the movement is mesmerizingly slow. And we experience the culmination of loss, longing, vulnerability, desire, and anticipation in the final twenty-nine minutes of the film. Gold flickers on blue where sun meets sea.

Jenkins's award-winning film is told in three acts, each representing a stage of the protagonist's progression from childhood to adulthood. Act 1 is titled Little, act 2 Chiron, and the final act is titled Black. We are to follow Chiron through the labyrinth of subjectivities he experiences, from tortured child to guarded teenager, and finally hardened adult, with all of the complexities of sexual discovery mixed in along the way. The three acts visually replicate three genres of film photography: Fuji, Agfa, and Kodak, and thus appear as deep saturation (act 1), muted tones (act 2), and warm, sumptuous light (act 3).[2] Act 3 functions as haptic, as the space between analog film and fingertip, fabric against skin.

In what feels akin to a collective nostalgic release, the film closes with the blue black of Little (played by Alex R. Hibbert)

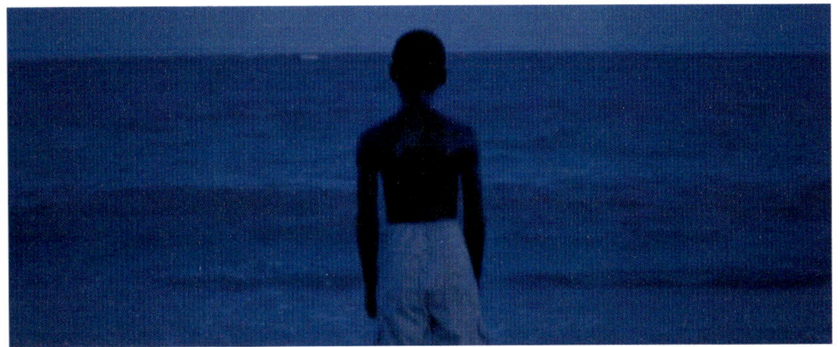

Figure 3.2
Barry Jenkins, dir., *Moonlight*, A24 / Plan B Entertainment, 2016.

against the darkening sky, the night blue sky against his dark skin. And we exhale. He looks forward. He looks back. The quest is now left in our hands. In a film that shimmers, immersed in color and tone, music registers as the sonic counterpoint. Touch, then, rounds out a purely sensorial experience that *Moonlight* illuminates. I'm interested in *Moonlight*'s haptical-ity, particularly as it mediates the space between looking and longing for Chiron and Kevin. Within this, we have the measure of the mark of queer desire, the fragile recognition of black interiority, and the force of cinema's still life. "There is power in looking," bell hooks writes.[3] Power. Release. Recognition. Affinity. Freedom. Affection. All this and more is set against a blue (Kevin) / gold (Chiron) background, framing the gaze and its expectant response in a cadence that flows like water on the Atlantic.

The blue tones that signal flashpoints of safety for Chiron are intermittent gestures of recognition that tell him he will be okay. The ocean is another signifier of desire, even as it is also present during the adolescent violence that marks the second act. When Black begins his journey to Kevin, the road merges with the dusk into the Atlantic where a group of children frolic with playful abandon. Chiron's evolution, battle made and hard won, is a tautly held enclosure that necessitates time to fully uncover. And since he is also recovering from childhood trauma and practicing forgiveness, he is a figure to be handled gently and with the recognition of vulnerability that precedes him like an ellipsis in the middle of a narrative description. In his quest for haptic regard, Chiron first visits his mother at a treatment center where she is working on her recovery. She is his first relationship with the distrust of tenderness and touch, and while he was a child she produced violence and tenderness in equal measure. Black is there to retrieve and hold onto what she can offer him in in this moment that is devoid of harm. They mourn together in this scene—what could have been—and try to find a way forward without violations of trust. Black's tears, his tenderness, sensitivity, and empathy return us to the quiet softness that he exudes in the first and second acts of the film.

"You ain't gotta love me," Paula tells Black as he holds back tears, "But you gon' know that I love you. You hear?," she asks as Black loses against the tear streaming down his face. "You hear me, Chiron," Paula continues. "I hear you, mama, he responds."[4] The exchange between them ends with Paula apologizing for the way she failed Black. And softness returns as they embrace in a circle of blue hues—Paula's shirt—Black's shirt—the chairs in the recovery center—and the blue sky—that points Black in the direction of Miami and Kevin.

My interest in *Moonlight* as a study in stillness is twofold: It assists in a photographic endeavor of black study (still life but with a photographic trace instead of a painterly one), and stillness as sonic practice where the body holds and allows sound to fill the space. To saturate it with intention (somewhere between Tina Campt's "thingyness" articulation in *Listening to Images* and Roy DeCarava's meditations in *The Sound I Saw*). To this I'd like to add haptic regard, or the look that touches. For in this work I am interested in how black regard functions when the white gaze is not a part of the consideration. If we, as Jenkins insists, "keep going," what might there be for us to see?

In the triptych display of Chiron's progressive evolution (from Little, to Chiron, to Black) Kevin is the center of his longing and part of the mechanistic production of loss. Through each of his stages Chiron is one of few words, making his careful, slow gestures part of the nuanced offering he shares with those in his very small circle. The film opens with actor Mahershala Ali, in an Academy Award-winning role, as Juan, coaxing Little from his hiding space (where he has run to escape bullies). Juan feeds Little, counsels him, and when the child is ready, brings him home to his mother. The transformation from stranger to mentor and father figure is encapsulated in act 1 of the film, but hovers everywhere after since Juan is deceased in the following two acts of the film. This means the one man in his life, consistent with tenderness and safety, exists in Little's early memory. The rest is longing and grief, unfolding over the film's temporal framework. We get a sense of Chiron's grief in the gestural motions of a trauma-infused recovery, the nuance of his corporeality.

Kevin occupies space in all three acts of the film's narrative arc, though intimacy and absence dominate the second act where Chiron experiences desire, vulnerability, and sexual awakening alongside violence and rejection. Michael Boyce Gillespie writes: "*Moonlight* conjures black becoming through the accented lens of survivors, black masculinities, and queer desires."[5] This becoming is both a looking at and a looking through, a mirroring apparatus that sutures one to another in the interactive atmosphere of human engagement. *I see you. I hear you. I feel you.* "What to do when there really is *no future*," Jafari Allen asks. "When death and nonbeing are imminent realities and not profound theorizations and understandable reflections of depressed public affect? Feel deeply. Fight to be seen for the future. And love fuck hate rage laugh work and twirl, *alively*, in the present."[6] Alively in the present is the quest that "keeps going" when the map bleeds off the page, offering a now that leaves room for the past and its potential future. "Aliveness," Kevin Quashie asserts, "is inevitable because it is *totality*, a black world rendering that implies neither universality nor prescription . . . but instead refers to everything of being in a black world."[7] *Aliveness* measures the space between here, over there, and an intimate adjacency that stitches one soul to the rest of the world. *Moonlight* is an offering of "aliveness" in light and dark, held or set free.

Losses are multiple for Chiron, from the haunting absence of parental neglect to the aggressive and sustained bullying he receives at school. By act 2, in what facilitates a break between them, Kevin's physical attack on Chiron sets his path forward through the violence of touch, marking the teenager with both gestures of haptic regard in equal fashion: the kiss, the punch. As we see later, Black is held together by very few threads, and by the film's end he is coiled so tightly that the last twenty minutes of the film hold the viewer in a suspended state of anticipation.

In the extensive exchange of glances and gazes, Kevin's intentional hold on Black is one part flirtation, and two parts curiosity. His body moves openly and freely. He is a book imaginatively displayed for the right group of readers. Importantly,

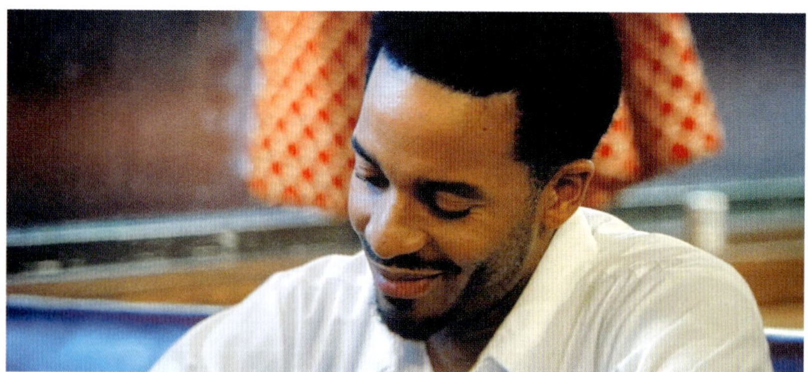

Figure 3.3
Intricacies of Kevin's haptic regard.

Kevin endears the viewer with the comfort he has with himself. It's a softened counterpoint to Chiron, or Black, who appears almost as a secret made flesh in the diner, hovering and quiet, and wresting time negotiating the space between longing and release. Kevin's gestures are an offering, as if he has been waiting forever, as if he has been waiting a day. But it is Black, right at this moment, who is worthy of an extended gaze. In the temporal demarcation of their reunion, what is the measure of queer desire and how is it encased? "Now the character has to finally make a choice," Jenkins states. "Now Chiron has to sit there opposite someone who's actually allowing [him] the space."[8] In the scene that "keeps going," we have a close reading of what Gillespie calls "textured beauty and blackness." Jenkins allows this textured blackness to envelop the filmic space as part of the atmosphere of engagement that saturates as it relinquishes control.

Carl Philips's titular poem from his book *Silverchest* is the control relinquished as the lover and the loved come together in the same space and time.

Unafraid is what we were, I think, and then afraid,
though it mostly seemed otherwise. I opened my eyes,
I saw, I closed. I shut them.
                                                  The usual morning glories
twist up and through banks of gone-wild-by-now holly;
crickets for song, morphos for their glamour, which
is quiet—blue, and quiet . . .

You: the dark that nothing, not even the light, displaces.
You, who have been the single leaf that
won't stop tossing,
among the others.
For you.[9]

"Silverchest" opens with "Unafraid," and by the final line "For you," pulls the emotive charge of desire through the entire length of the poem, reaching up and outward, like the haptic gesture of the beloved. *Unafraid . . . For you . . .* The "blue, and quiet" is from Little to Juan and Black to Kevin, in a concentric circle of the oceanic that signals safety and understanding for Chiron in a language he understands. Water as immersive warmth, as route and return, stands as a beacon for Chiron that he can return to in a repetition of memory making, "the single leaf that / won't stop tossing" while he meanders through his adulthood with disciplined precision, but few comforts. Act 3 is the culmination of Black coming into being with the full measure of his humanity intact. In each scene he moves with aquatic precision, in the direction of desire. And for the sake of that desire. Because Black is steeped in the mourning arc that shaped him, because he walks with grief set against his chest, the film (and its photographic accompaniment) visually renders this hapticality with a stillness that is saturated so fully that one can feel it from one shot to another. It is this haptic quality of *Moonlight* that spares no subtlety, offering the viewer a look that touches in tender, careful, close caresses.

As they sit across from one another, Black flecked with gold—teeth, watch, necklace, and bracelet—the warmth of the light in the diner glistens against his skin. The diner empties

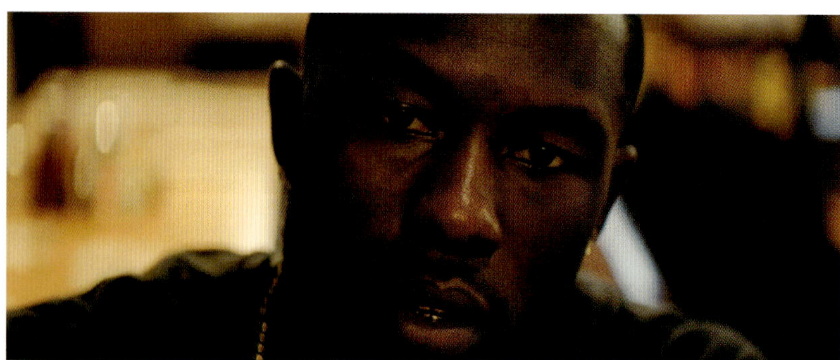

Figure 3.4
Barry Jenkins, dir., *Moonlight*, A24 / Plan B Entertainment, 2016.

out, giving Kevin and Black the opportunity to be more honest within their reunion, going past the requisite questions about how they are each doing and onto the more important matters of the heart and mind. Black glances at the door of the diner and silently decides he will say what he has been meaning to say.

BLACK “Why’d you call me?”

KEVIN “What?”

BLACK “Why’d you call me?”

KEVIN “I told you, man. Dude came in—”

BLACK “Yeah. Yeah. Yeah.”

KEVIN “He played this song, man.”

Kevin rises to play the song “Hello Stranger” by Barbara Lewis and in the interim Kevin and Black exchange the all-important gazes that hold their present and past selves with all of the complicated emotional trajectories they carry. Filmic enclosures extend this tenderness in venues (restaurants, automobiles, living spaces) that allow for the portrayal of intimacy to deepen the engagement at play. After Black agrees to drive Kevin to his apartment, they continue the conversation Black began when he entered the diner with desire on his sleeve, looking for a face from the past. As they arrive outside Kevin’s apartment Black is struck by the sound of the sea, the ocean of his childhood remembrance in the visceral framework his grief has taken. Because grief is his travel companion, Black exudes the fragility of mourning embedded within a body that is perceived as hard. As hardened. The blue flame of the stovetop meets Kevin’s sea blue shirt as he re-emerges from his bedroom to continue his conversation with Black. All else is flecked with gold/yellow in the apartment, from the walls to Kevin Jr.’s crayon drawings slicing the space between the two men as they confront their past together. Their past apart. While Black confesses to building himself up anew after their last interaction as teenagers, Kevin claims that he "just kept going" since that seemed like the easiest thing to do. Kevin confesses to Black that he is about to become the man he wants to be: "It's a life. I ain't never had that before." His ease and comfort is a trigger for Black, who has never achieved an ability to be a full and authentic version of himself. Not with others or alone. And Kevin's admission that what he currently has is enough emboldens Black to make an admission of his own. "You the only man that's ever touched me," he tells Kevin. "You the only one. I haven't really touched anyone since." Kevin turns to meet Black's gaze. To hold it there for as long as is necessary. To look with intention and interest, empathy, and care. Hard but soft, closed yet open. Fixed and malleable. Chiron says the words he has been holding onto like a secret to the only person it matters that he tell. Kevin's tender recognition is an enclosure that fills itself with the dimensions of complex personhood rendered with care. The journey from denial to desire is an ocean. An abyss. Sun, sea, river, mountain.

In *Jazz*, Dorcas hears drums at a parade in remembrance of her murdered mother and father. And for her, "the drums were not an all-embracing rope of fellowship, discipline and transcendence. She remembered them as a beginning, a start of something she looked to complete."[10] As she imagines it, a fleck of wood drifts out from the leftover ashes of the fire that consumed Dorcas's parents and "lodged comfortably somewhere below her navel," burning still. It was an ember, a "glow" that would be "waiting for and with her whenever she wanted to be touched by it."[11] And Dorcas is ruled by the god of touch.

When Dorcas and Felice make their way to a party "led straight to the right place more by the stride piano pouring over the door saddle than their recollection of the apartment number," they are eager to be in the communion of sight, sound, and touch.

> Under the ceiling light pairs move like twins born with, if not for, the other, sharing a partner's pulse like a second jugular. They believe

The journey from denial to desire is an ocean. An abyss. Sun, sea, river, mountain.

they know before the music does what their hands, their feet are to do, but that illusion is the music's secret drive: the control it tricks them into believing is theirs; the anticipation it anticipates. In between record changes, while the girls fan blouse necks to air damp collarbones or pat with anxious hands the damage moisture has done to their hair, the boys press folded handkerchiefs to their foreheads. Laughter covers indiscreet glances of welcome and promise, and takes the edge off gestures of betrayal and abandon.[12]

It is abandon they are after, and the ability to glide in and through the bustling crowd, insular in its rhythmic construction, with flesh grazing and caressing flesh. Without specifically articulating this need, the desire for touch, *Jazz* throbs with the silent knowing of the healing power of tenderness, of touch, and haptic regard. And so each character looks knowingly, curiously, at another, seeking out the familiar in the strange of each intimate encounter.

The flame of the ember grows, touched by the fire within, and fortified by regard that says "*you are there . . . because I am looking at you . . .*" in a circle of modulated understanding that deepens personal connections. Amanda Russhell Wallace's 2017 image *Ember* signals the distinctive remains of the beloved when they are both here and no longer. In a burnt orange background with ghostly contours gesturing to the absence of one who is lost, *Ember* carries the shape of the sound of the touch of grief.

Longing and loss are yoked together in Audre Lorde's book *Zami: A New Spelling of My Name: A Biomythography*. In it, Lorde reflects on her big and small intimacies. One of her earliest relationships is with Genevieve, a creative wild child Lorde meets in high school. They bond quickly and effortlessly, their shared vulnerabilities pulling them closer together as they negotiate the larger world around them, two by two. It's clear that as Lorde reflects on this time with Gennie, this reflection highlights the would-have-been that never got to be. Genevieve takes her own life amid the turmoil of a custody fight

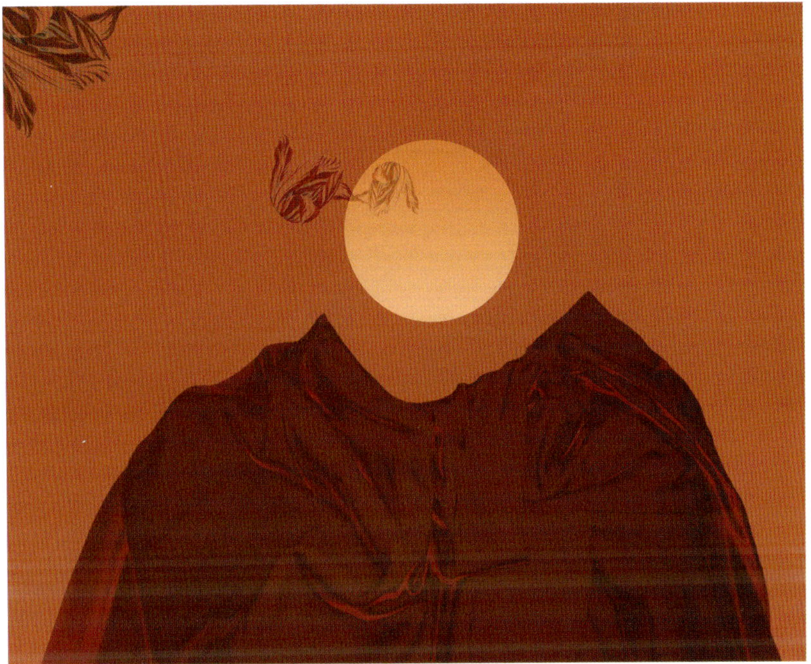

Figure 3.5
Amanda Russhell Wallace, *Ember*, 2017.

between her parents, having threatened to do so for months beforehand. Lorde, devastated by the loss, is a swirling list of wishes that the futurity of her relationship with Genevieve held out for her:

> Things I never did with Genevieve: Let our bodies touch and tell the passions that we felt. Go to a Village gay bar, or any bar anywhere. Smoke reefer. Derail the freight that took circus animals to Florida. Take a course in international obscenities. Learn Swahili. See Martha Graham's dance troupe. Visit Pearl Primus. Ask her to take us away with her to Africa next time. Write THE BOOK. Make love.[13]

Zami might be described as a product of proximity and of touch. Lorde's symbolic examination hovers between spaces and bodies. The memoir emphasizes how women—Lorde's mother, along with others in her life including Gennie, Ginger, Bea, Eudora, Felice, Muriel, Rhea, etc.,—all form part of the center of the author's self-made universe. This universe is a map of ntimacy and identity, with Lorde navigating the space between love and loss through her friends and lovers, her family, and her body. Lorde wrote *Zami* while battling breast cancer. Along with *Sister Outsider* and *The Cancer Journals*, *Zami* unfolds as a multilayered exploration of autonomous existence. *Zami* is, at its center, a quest for connection that is facilitated through touch. In it, Lorde negotiates the difficult space between love and profound, repetitive loss. Her river. Her mountain. Amber Jamilla Musser writes: "Lorde's insistence on having sensuality, desire, woman loving, and politics meet in the same space is deliberate. The radicality of insisting on a language of sex for queer black female bodies rescripts the ways that coalition might be enacted; it renders the sensual political in large part because this queer feminine . . . offers a challenge to the epistemologies of sexuality."[14] Lorde locates her quest as a journey through touch—tentative, fragile, passionate, tortured—draped over the consequential years of her life. Published two years after *The Cancer Journals*, *Zami* pulls the disparate pieces of Lorde's corporeality into a cohesive, erotic, intimate whole. Understanding her body in its state of cancerous inflection point, Lorde reflects on her relationships in order to acknowledge, like Coltrane's *A Love Supreme*, what has made her who she is—dissonance and assonance—as she grapples with all she has lost and all she has learned. Lorde's poetry never leaves her, and neither does her insistence upon her connections, the life pulse of ability to "do language" and conjure the dead. "To be sensual, I think," James Baldwin wrote, "is to respect and rejoice in the force of life, of life itself, and to be present in all that one does, from the effort of loving to the breaking of bread."[15] Because the reader moves with her on her journeys, from poetry to prose, fury to passion, we bear witness to Lorde's command of word and deed as she endeavors to make herself known.

Rebecca Hall's filmic adaptation of Nella Larsen's 1929 novel *Passing* also traverses the space between saturation and control for Irene (played by Tessa Thompson) and her childhood friend, Clare (played by Ruth Negga). The film beautifully captures much of the sexual tension imbued in the novel, as passing, as metaphor, opens a series of transgressions for two black cosmopolitan women who find themselves betwixt and between America's peculiar one-drop color line. Clare passes for white in this world, and Irene, for the most part, does not.

In the lush landscape of the film's framing, Irene's quest to move through Clare manifests itself upon their first encounter after so many years apart. Clare is looking and Irene is glancing. Clare holds her gaze until Irene can no longer look away. Her body. The poise. The deep breathing. The look that does not stop looking. James Elkins writes, "In life a gaze challenges, it inquires, it takes pleasure and it asks for a response."[16] And so a dance of call-and-response is an invitation between two people who know the danger and look anyway. The loss of intimacy between the film's two protagonists is a callback to a past where they could coexist with their desires exposed to the light. In the furtive glances at the film's center, Hall directs the line of sight from the heart pulse out, as Clare and Irene attempt to return to the world they left behind. *Because I am looking at you . . .*

Using the brim of her hat as a shield, Irene sits alone at the Drayton, having stopped for a cool drink in an establishment she knows is marked for whites only. She is careful, poised, and hypervigilant concerning her surroundings. Observing all around her—a woman whose body is visually obscured, a couple performing the ritual of public affection, and two elderly women siting together, one sipping tea while the other gazes off into the distance. The two women are proximate to each other but seemingly worlds apart—as detached as two gentle yet opposing forces navigating the same space. Irene's eyes continue to meander. They move across and back, past the seated figure holding Irene in her elegant gaze. Clare. Irene sets her eyes downward, apprehensive and tentative. Clare's eyes do not let go. Irene rises to leave, likely mistaking Clare's gaze for racial scrutiny. "And there was about her an amazing soft malice," Larsen writes, "hidden well away until provoked."[17] Irene provokes devoid of intention, for it is the sight of her, the surprise reunion that sends Clare's impulsive fire to full flame. Across the table from her childhood friend, Clare reaches for Irene's hand, touches it, while Irene instinctively pulls away. Clare lights a cigarette—her fire, her flame—and prods Irene's hesitance. "Well, we can see lots of one another these days that I'm here, can't we?" Irene isn't so sure.

Passing replicates the haptic quality of black-and-white photography alongside the aesthetic enclosures that signal intimacy and interiority. Hall's rendering of the slippages and constraints of identity brings a visceral tacticity to Irene and Clare's reunion. After the series of gazes and glances between the two women, Clare glides over to Irene's table with intention.

CLARE "Pardon me. I don't mean to stare, but I think I know you."

IRENE "I'm afraid you're mistaken."

CLARE "No, of course I know you, Rene. You look just the same. Tell me, do they still call you Rene?"

IRENE "Yes. Though no one's called me that for a long time."

CLARE "Don't you know me? Not really Rene?"

IRENE "I'm afraid I can't seem to place . . . Clare?"[18]

From "Why'd you call me?" to "Don't you know me?," longing floats in a cinematic spiral that leads, dangerously even, in the direction of desire. Clare and Irene's reunion is filled with intensity, caution, trepidation, and fascination. Though their collective hunger spills out to separate results and

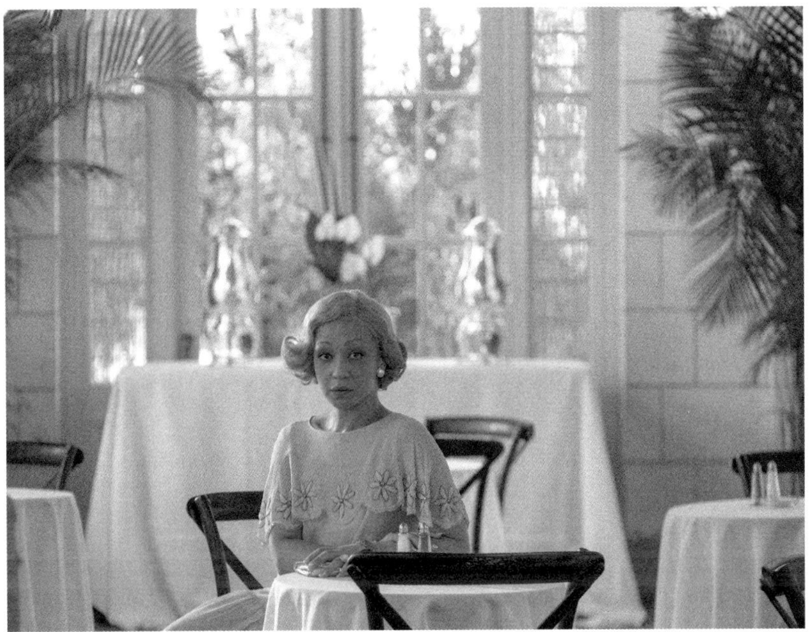

Figure 3.6
Rebecca Hall, dir., *Passing*, Picture Films / Netflix Studios, 2021.

possibilities, both women are encased in the respectable compartments that keep them from holding one another close. The film manages the fraught boundary between race, sexuality, geography, and desire by using Irene and Clare as magnets unable to look away from each other once their eyes meet. Touch, though risky for both, is nevertheless attempted within the confines of their bodies as separate, as same.

Both *Passing* and *Moonlight* possess configurations of analog photography, and in this they are drawing on the aesthetic referral of photography's haptic materiality. "If a photograph's frequencies are a potential route to a different kind of knowledge," Michèle Pearson Clarke writes, "a knowledge generated by feeling—then perhaps the rough texture, the

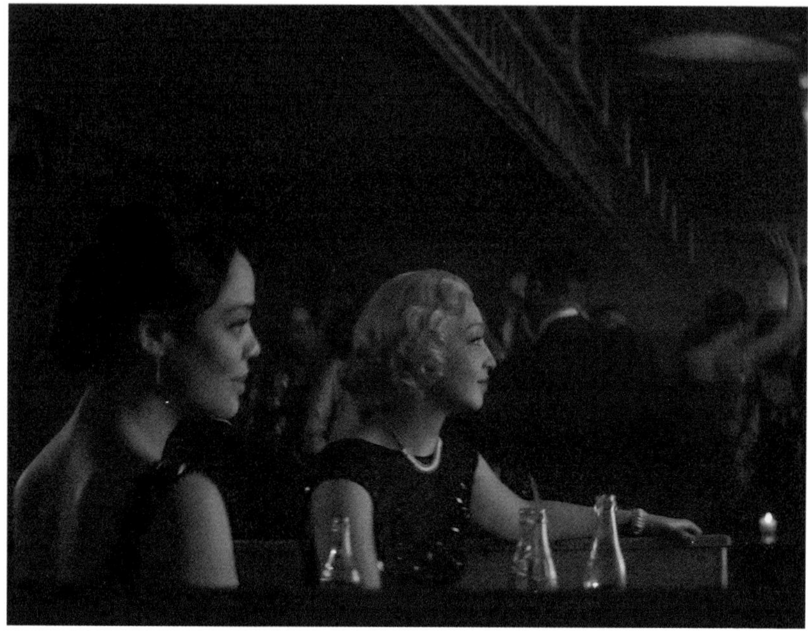

Figure 3.7
Rebecca Hall, dir., *Passing*, Picture Films / Netflix Studios, 2021.

'thingyness' of an analogue photograph of Blackness produces an intensity of vibrations to which we can more easily attune."[19] This ability to attune is accentuated by both motion and stillness. And for both films, it is a study in the gravitational pull that is imbricated by longing *as* loss. Longing as release.

Dell Marie Hamilton's *Emulsions in Departure* features fingers on photographic print, painted with haptic regard and vigilant longing. Forming part of Hamilton's early work, *Emulsions in Departure* is a film/photography interplay that uses the imprint of Hamilton's fingers to provide texture and tone to the materiality of loss. Of longing. A fortunate accident while scanning images produced the series, which has the visual effect of merging all of the elements into a series of photographic prints. Earth, wind, fire, and water converge here, as constitutive constructions of the black diaspora separated by oceans, rivers, and seas. Hamilton's abstraction is also a submersion, deepening the discourse of loss that carries itself across terrains in order to render grief visible even if it is only partially legible to others. With the title *Emulsions in Departure*, Hamilton engenders an atmosphere of separation amid convergence, where mourning often resides. Referring to the work as "melancholy," Hamilton's use of texture and color creates a parallel engagement wherein an architecture of grief flows outward and provides a visual dispersal that coheres around the disparate subjectivities of black life. Emulsions signify the touch of liquid on liquid, mist on mist, in order to bond and separate with intention. This *touch on touch* is put in the service of haptic layering for Hamilton, who mixes and merges her art process so that it follows her aesthetic design. In her effort to bind memory to image making, *Emulsions* brings the anxiety of separation into a tactile canvas of artistic management.

Departures saturate Jafari S. Allen's *There's a Disco Ball Between Us: A Theory of Black Gay Life*, and it is at times overwhelming to place in context, in time. In the archive of black grief and black artistic production there is the "material and/or ethereal evidence—burnt shards, traces of the violence: your playlists, meeting agendas, eviction notices, and the first draft of your grant proposal" to reference the work that is done and that is yet to be done.[20] The work yet to be done includes that of the haptic retrieval, which can attempt to measure losses we are just now beginning to calculate. Reverberations of HIV/AIDS haptic refusals drift into more contemporary discourses of COVID while detaching the latter from an explicit marker of sexual identity. "Many of the scenes and many of the people who made the still-significant long 1980s fierce have already passed," Allen writes. "My preoccupation, pace Morrison, is that it seems they have also been *passed on* in too many ways."[21] If "this is not a story to pass on" then it is also a not

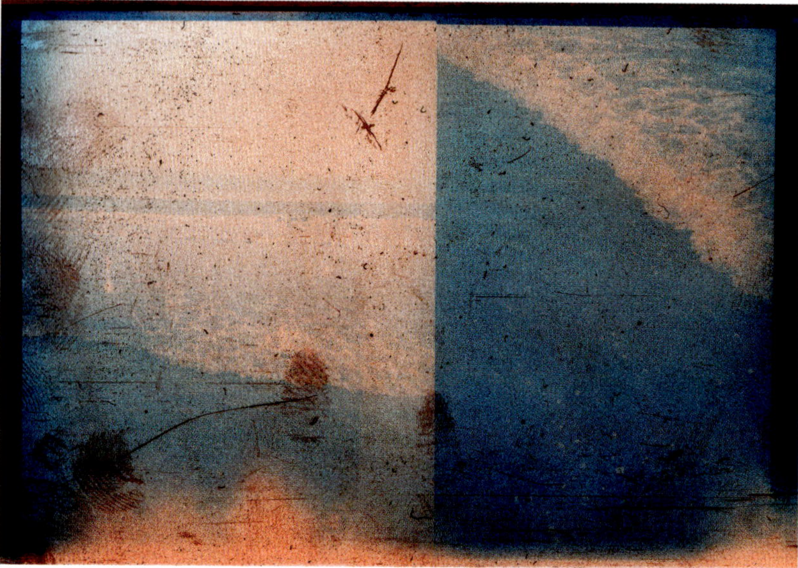

Figure 3.8
Dell Marie Hamilton, *Emulsions in Departure #12* (shot in 2010, printed in 2016). Courtesy of the artist.

a story to "pass on," and this is how we can hold the gaze on offer and return it with understanding and communion.

Carrie Mae Weems's 2016 video *People of a Darker Hue* brings together images and archival sound clips with Weems's melodic voice-over in order to compel the viewer in a mesmerizing sweep of black presence and black being. Weems melds her artistic concerns into a sight/sound navigation bound by touch. With dozens of mostly black subjects moving about on city streets in the first section, the viewer is immersed in a swirl of slow-paced migration that intimates slow-paced racial progress. A voice-over by Paul Robeson duplicates the sound of black mourning amid black revolution as Robeson delineates the point of his navigational trajectory:

I am today giving up my concerts for two or three years to enter into this struggle at a very . . . it's what I call getting into the rank and file struggle of my people for full citizenship in these United States. So I won't be singing except for the rights of my people for the next couple of years. No pretty songs gentleman, no pretty songs. Time for some full citizenship.

Understandable, the attempt of the enemy was to cut off the progressive people from the great masses of the Americans. In my own case it was to cut me off from the Negro people from whom I was born. Imagine, somewhere somebody says, I, born a Negro, that because of my beliefs, my fight for peace, my fight for friendship between nations, my fight for the complete liberation of my people, that somewhere I am not an American. That I should be cut off from the very people from whom I was born.[22]

Weems's voice enters, overlapping with Robeson's. Set against a blue background and the image of a single figure running in place, we hear Weems again present a series of statistics ("he was 39 . . . she was 25 . . . she was 34 . . . he was 27 . . . he was 12") until they merge in a repetition that signals the unrelenting violence of white supremacy. Out of this auditory enclosure comes the visual duplication of people engaged in the act of mourning even as the acts they have assembled to protest continue. Midway through the video we see black subjects, placing open hands against their chests, eyes closed, and collectively grieving the lives lost that Weems outlines in her vocal arrangement. The scene is split with archival video clips of recorded murders from Laquan McDonald to Philando Castile and Eric Garner. For LaCharles Ward, "acting as visual transitions, so to speak, the protestors return with clinched fists hitting their chests as to signal the continual outcry against each act of violence."[23] It is this visual act, then, that provides the heartbeat of the video, bringing the gesture of intimacy of touch toward a collective goal.

As Weems highlights the work of communion in witnessing and participates in an artistic laying on of hands, *People*

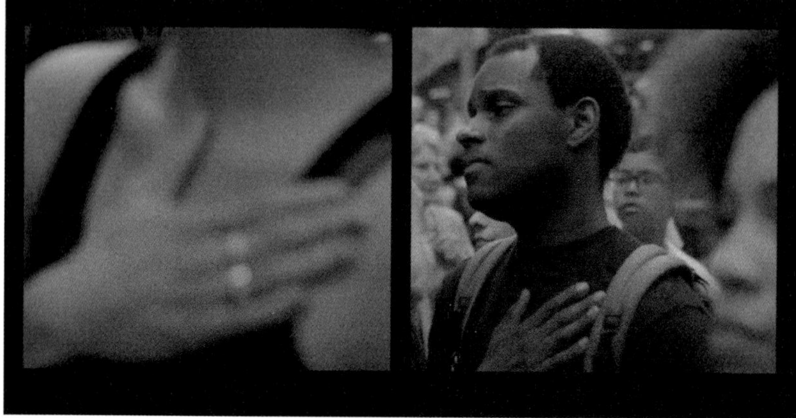

Figure 3.9
Carrie Mae Weems, *People of a Darker Hue* (video still), 2016. © Carrie Mae Weems. Courtesy of the artist and Gladstone Gallery, New York, Fraenkel Gallery, San Francisco, and Galerie Barbara Thumm, Berlin.

of a Darker Hue also succeeds in modulating the fragile space between one black subject and another in the arena of external world racializations and the violence that greets those who are rendered available to indiscriminate extraction. The images remind the viewer that the space between one and another is a vulnerable space, a fragile liminality that asks for vigilance in the face of black exposure to danger. For as Weems states:

> They were no strangers to sorrow. Time and time again, the man was rejected, the woman was denied. A man was killed, the body laid in the open, uncovered and exposed. Women wailed and men moaned. For reasons unknown, I saw him running. I saw him stop. I saw him turn with raised hands. I heard a shot. I saw him fall. For reasons unknown, I rejected my own knowledge and I deceived myself by refusing to believe that this was possible.[24]

People of a Darker Hue, Weems seems to say, cannot separate themselves from the limited frame of seeing and being seen exhibited by others. They, too, must participate in haptic regard, and do so with an emphasis that returns the body back to itself, extends the contours of recognition, and offers haptic testimony to all and any who've been lost.

Jazz ends with the unnamed narrator ruminating on the contours of love, of touch, that animate her ability to provide testimony to the arc of intimacy she witnesses and of which she wants to take part. In this, she functions as a representation of collective desire, as she endeavors to release herself of the burdens of desire. Of Joe and Violet Trace, she admits:

> I envy them their public love. I myself have only known it in secret, shared it in secret and longed, aw longed to show it—to be able to say out loud what they have no need to say at all: *That I have loved only you, surrendered my whole self reckless to you and nobody else. That I want you to love me back and show it to me. That I love the way you hold me, how close you let me be to you. I like your fingers on and on, lifting, turning. I have watched your face for a long time now, and missed your eyes when you went away from me. Talking to you and hearing you answer—that's the kick.*
>
> But I can't say that aloud; I can't tell anyone that I have been waiting for this all my life and that being chosen to wait is the reason I can. If I were able I'd say it. Say make me, remake me. You are free to do it and I am free to let you because look, look. Look where your hands are. Now.[25]

Now. Now. In the immediacy of the haptic, in the "dark that nothing, not even the light, displaces," is the doubling elegy of longing and loss. Each character in the novel navigates this loss and longing differently. From Violet who flails trying to reach back to the person she could have been, to Joe who embraced his former training as a hunter to disastrous results, to Felice who settled into her dismissive trace of mourning for a friend. Alice Manfred tried to restrict her way out of the danger that accompanies an acknowledgment of grief. And she

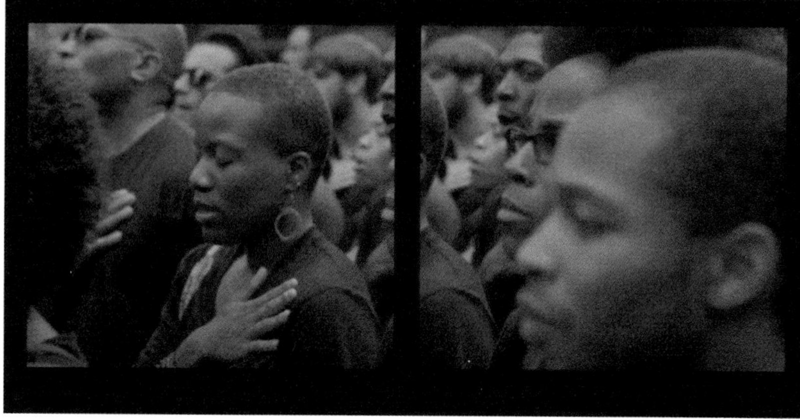

Figure 3.10
Carrie Mae Weems, *People of a Darker Hue* (video still), 2016. © Carrie Mae Weems. Courtesy of the artist and Gladstone Gallery, New York, Fraenkel Gallery, San Francisco, and Galerie Barbara Thumm, Berlin.

tried to restrict her niece Dorcas so that eventually the apartment they shared together began to close in on Dorcas like the lid of a coffin. Morrison's novel is a reminder of the movement that grief takes, who it holds and what it won't let go. And the book invites the reader in from the very beginning of the opening ("Sth, I know that woman") to the final line, "Now." It gestures toward the grandeur of the ease of understanding that intimacy retrieves if you let it. And the immediacy of the visceral embodiment of a love that is there "for you."

CODA: GRIEF IN THE DARK

If I tried to write a universal novel, it would be water.

—Toni Morrison

One body moves in sync and in time with another. Together they bend to the arc of the wind and the sun. The attendant percussion, its rhythms and heartbeat swell with the flow of the crowd. Be it large or small, the energy of the crowd illuminates and heightens the work taking place. The Brazilian art of capoeira, one-part martial art, one part dance, is the work of forced improvisation—a hybrid negotiation between resistance and symmetry. It makes proximate the violence of touch without reproducing the violence of that touch. Intimate and elegantly coordinated, the practitioners bring their bodies into conversation with the grief that abides enslavement, and aids survival.

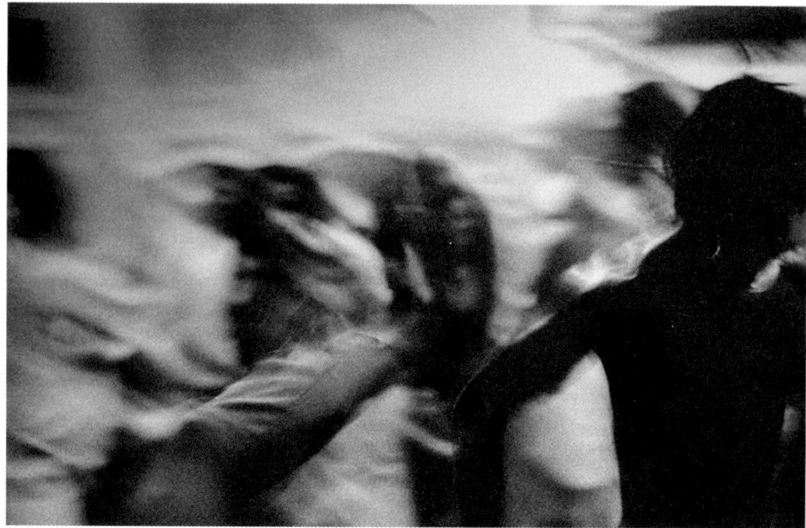

Figure 4.1
Brazilian capoeira performance, Salvador da Bahia, Brazil, 2005. Photograph by the author.

If we can glean, in the *almost-touch* of capoeira, the boundless resistance of the sorrow song, the drumbeat/heartbeat of ecstatic release, we will have some sense of the measure of corporeal response located here. It feels like witnessing the coexisting energies that feed off each other, and then into the crowd around them. A force field created in its ephemeral production, and encircling those in want, those in need.

The origins of Brazilian capoeira are located in Angola, and are transported to Brazil via the transatlantic slave trade that the Portuguese originated in the fifteenth century. We know much about the violent dehumanizing process of Portuguese enslavement, and how aggressively it was maintained—until the cusp of the twentieth century, no less—but individual and collective acts of resistance are embedded in the sights and sounds of the nation. Even more so in the inscribed movements of the tens of millions of descendants of the

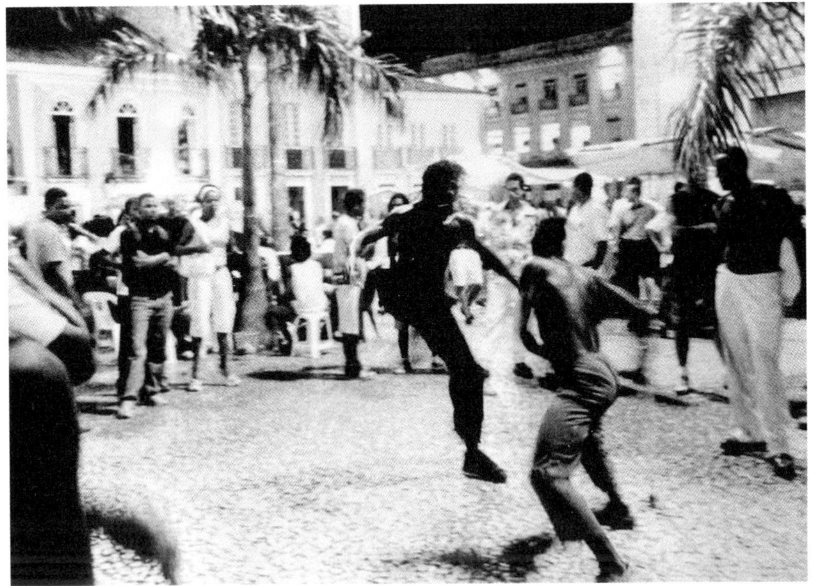

Figure 4.2
Brazilian capoeira performance. Photograph by the author.

transatlantic slave trade whose geographical endpoint from Middle Passage ships was the South American colony of the Portuguese empire.

In Salvador da Bahia, former capital of the nation of Brazil, on the edge of the Bay of All Saints, there sits a lasting monument to the long legacy of slavery that we still don't fully understand in its totality. But all the senses converge in Salvador, if you are paying close enough attention. And all the sounds respond to the cacophony of grief encircling its atmosphere. Lá, in the center of the bustling city, on a lake forged from the past, orishas standing twenty-two feet tall conjure souls. They float, with armor and shield, closer to the heavens from which they source their power. They rise, like the undead, from the body of water that formerly held a seventeenth-century dam.

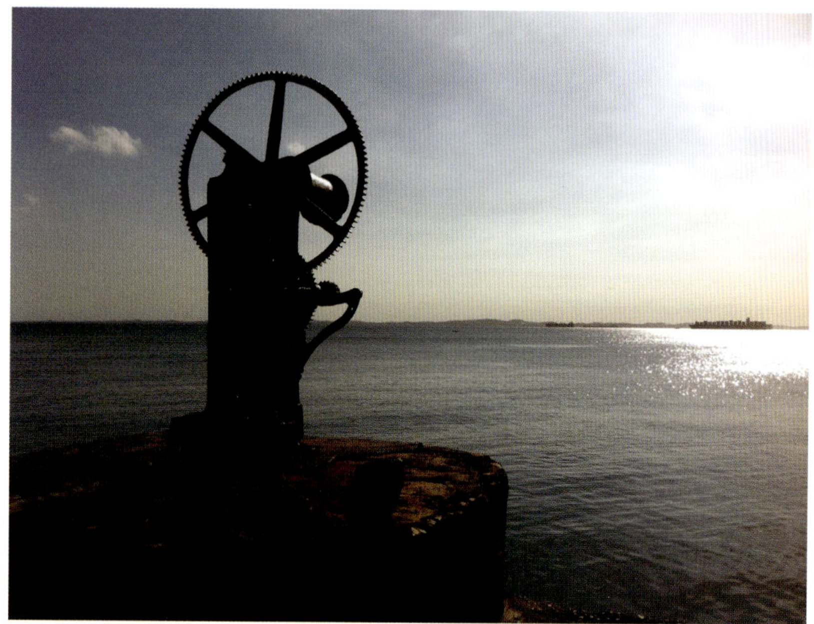

Figure 4.3
Museu de Arte Moderna da Bahia.
Photograph by the author.

So, for nearly four hundred years of Portuguese imperialism this aquatic center held the secrets and now reveals them in the circular formation of a protective ecstatic shield. The first slave market in the new world, the site of a military embankment, the resurrection site for Yoruba deities, and the spiritual heartbeat of the nation, Salvador da Bahia is also home to the remnants of sugar plantations that signal the country's previous relationship to the source of its early wealth. And in the motions and movements of Brazilian art and dance, we see the residue of forced improvisation rendered artistically.

Like a sorrow song with a double meaning, slavery's temporal boundaries and geographic portals teach us how to navigate the *after* of this violent *before*. In the Caribbean and

South America, cultural retentions combine with New World mourning rituals to help keep black subjects from drifting into despair. An entire universe of catharsis and control, ritual and memory is produced through the wonders of creative expression that are tethered to this history. Though I have mostly focused on the United States in my exploration of these elegies, we know how expansive this productive extension is because the Atlantic Ocean, that vast waterway that invented the black diaspora, is its most defining feature.

Dionne Brand writes, "Water is the first thing in my memory. The sea sounded like a thousand secrets, all whispered at the same time. In the daytime it was indistinguishable to me from air. It seemed to be made of the same substance. The same substance which carried voices or smells, music or emotion."[1] Water as ecstatic elixir, which facilitates the verisimilitude of flow—flow as glide, as sway, as air-guided journey that moves, in the words of Lucille Clifton "from this to that." In its temporal elongation the ocean, the sea, has stood as elemental witness to the vagaries of humanity, as its relationship to life has been investigated, drained, poisoned, and pillaged. "All beginning in water. All ending in water," Brand reminds us. In its endurance and malleability there is much to discover, much to discern. In the molecular composition that is two parts hydrogen and one part oxygen, an entire world exists. For the expansive range of movement embedded in the oceanic we understand "the sea was its own country, its own sovereign."[2] The sea beguiles and hypnotizes, meanders and remains. In order to grapple with its potency and its special contours, attention must be paid to the black diasporic reference points that are made in its name. And in its wake. The sea encompasses humanity's original declaration of existence, and by inference, its end.

Before I made my way to Thomas Jefferson's plantation home, I visited Salvador da Bahia for research. The whole city is a merging of slavery, spirituality, music, grief, and celebration. As a resonant "city of the dead," Brazil, according to

In its temporal elongation the ocean, the sea, has stood as elemental witness to the vagaries of humanity, as its relationship to life has been investigated, drained, poisoned, and pillaged.

Joseph Roach, "derives from its ghostly power to insinuate memory between the lines, in the spaces between the words, in the intonation and placement by which they are shaped, in the silences by which they are deepened or contradicted. By such means, the dead remain among the living."[3] In Salvador da Bahia, the dead and the living cohere in order to shape the memory of slavery and mourn in plain sight. What the landscape and terrain of slave plantations in the United States offered, Brazil does through the Atlantic.

When Salvador de Bahia's famous musical group *Didá Banda Feminina* emerge to perform on Tuesday evenings in Pelourinho's central square, their audience is engaging with the visual remains of Portuguese slavery. Each member of the Afro-Brazilian group appears wearing an outfit replete with the image of the slave deity Blessed Anastácia across her chest, her symbolic violated and enslaved body serving a cultural and historical purpose. As the young women move, their drumming, singing, and dancing bodies work in silent dedication to a powerful historical enigma. As Afro-Brazilians wrestle with slavery's unmistakable intimacy with death, Anastácia gives them visual appeasement. The slave woman is offered up as an entity able to transcend her earthly body for the benefit of all who descend from slavery's racialized underclass. The visual image of the deity, taken from a nineteenth-century sketch by a French traveler, shows the contemporary incarnation of collective intention. Whereas Jacques Arago drew the figure of a male slave being punished in Colonial Rio de Janeiro, Brazilians over a century later witnessed a miracle of gender transference in flesh and image when they found the sketch in a museum in 1968. She is their creation. They have yet to let her go.

Pelourinho is a Brazilian Portuguese word that means pain—slave pain. Translated as "pillory," there is the remnant of a whipping post in the central square of the former capital city that now negotiates the physical terrain of deities and dancers, imagery and memory. This project, despite its preoccupations, is not about death, but rather an examination of the denial of vulnerability negotiated by black Atlantic subjects since antiblackness is routinely made palatable so that the past continually informs the present. This is a phenomenon that takes place rigidly and repeatedly on black bodies, like the musicians who enter Pelourinho's center every Tuesday evening, mere steps away from one of Brazil's more successful slave markets and torture stages. The musicians face their audience carrying the grief of the violent embodiment of the past, informed by deep, abiding loss.

And so, though I made my first journey to Brazil searching for the pinprick of slavery's remains, I left consumed by the specter of ghosts. I saw faces that so resembled my own they felt like kin. I watched movements of bodies that seemed steeped in a kind of unspoken understanding, a ballet of dark recognition. I spent days gazing out at the Atlantic and finding a kind of soothing unease, as if I had been drawn to the water in that particular space so my body could feel the waves against my skin. Waves that felt like loss, felt like home, and felt like love.

Waves that felt like loss, felt like home, and felt like love.

ACKNOWLEDGMENTS

To study slavery is to consider grief in all its permutations, grief in the expansive interiority of black life. In this book, I have gone everywhere these elegies have taken me. All journeys, no matter how winding or circular, lead somewhere. I am fortunate that this journey has led me here, and this is in no small part due to those with whom I have come into contact. To Victoria Hindley at the MIT Press, my gratitude knows no limit, for you have ushered this project from its infancy to its fruition. I thank you for that. To the rest of the MIT/Brown University Digital Publications team: Allison Levy, Gabriela Bueno Gibbs, Nicholas DiSabatino, Holiday Shapiro, Olivia Lafferty, Kathleen Caruso, Crystal Brusch, Julia Collins, and Jennifer Braga—thank you for the care you have shown me while I made my way through this work. To the anonymous reviewers of the manuscript, I thank you for the time you have given to the project and the suggestions that have made their way into the final product.

Black Elegies began as a curated set of images/texts for the CARE SYLLABUS module at MASS MoCA. I thank Victoria Papa and Levi Prombaum for the invitation to think through some of the sites of grief I have highlighted in this book. I have presented portions of *Black Elegies* at Emory University, Dartmouth College (Futures of American Studies), Harvard University, the American Studies Association, McGill University, Brown University, Black Portraitures (Paris), and Yale University. I have received funding for *Black Elegies* from the Graham Foundation for Advanced Studies in the Fine Arts, and a fellowship from the Hutchins Center for African & African American Research at Harvard University. The time and resources these awards have afforded me cannot be overstated. I am incredibly lucky and so very grateful they arrived when they did. At the Hutchins Center, I was in great company, spurred on by fellows who were brilliant and generous, kind, and intentional. In addition to Henry Louis Gates Jr. and Krishna Winston, my thanks to Rashauna Johnson, Reighan Gillam, Nii Ayikwei Parkes, Faith Lois Smith, Antônia Gabriela Pereira de Araùjo, Paul Tiyambe Zeleza, Stevie "Dr. View" Johnson, Mandy Izadi, David "Dee-1" Augustine, Shirley Moody-Turner, Celeste-Marie Bernier, Jim Downs, Jorge Delgadillo Núñez, Panashe Chigumadzi, Tamary Kudita, Aabid Allibhai, Rhae Lynn Barnes, K'Naan Warsame, and Nancy Jacobs. During my Hutchins Center presentation, Emily Greenwood offered the word I had been searching for as I considered the range of this archive: "ecstasy," and this allowed me to delve into the project anew.

Dartmouth College is enjoyable in no small part due to the following people, and I thank them for it: Naaborko Sackeyfio-Lenoch, Vievee Francis, Shontay Delalue, Adedoyin Teriba, Jénee Potts, Kianna Middleton, Donald Pease, Kianny Antigua, Shaonta' Allen, Jorge Cuellar, Alexander Chee, Bailey Thomas, Jane Henderson, Carolyn Dever, Jermaine Wilcox, Trica Keaton, Matthew Olzmann, Mary Coffey, Endia Hayes, Jami Powell, Alysia Garrison, Tanya Edwards, Dean Madden, Ella Bell Smith, Charlotte Bacon, Allie Martin, Kate Gibbel, Susan

Brison, Ingrid Brioso Rieumont, Alisa Swindell, Colleen Glenney Boggs, Tricia Treacy, Iyabo Kwayana, Mauricio Acuña, Peter Orner, Melisa (Meli) Zeiger, Jodi Kim, and Chloe Poston: what a rural posse we are! I am and will forever be indebted to the students in my Black Elegies seminar. Their profound and deeply generative analyses held these varied texts together like a poem in free verse.

My friends, family, and my chosen kin have sustained me throughout this process and I cannot thank them enough. To Vanessa Monique Liles I owe an innate sense of justice, joy, and regal earthiness. Vanessa accompanied me to various slave plantations throughout the U.S. South, and held her faith in the history of human perseverance. Shirley Carrie Hartman practices deep thought and deep care for those she loves. I am lucky to count myself among them. Nadine Adjoa Smith has been a sustaining force in my life for twenty-five years, and now along with Ayo Jumoke I hope that we continue to make heart space and time for each other as always. To Sandy Alexandre (and Zora Felice)—all the best things and in boisterous abundance. Fatima El-Tayeb, Eunsong Kim, Michael Chaney, Lisa Lowe, Helen Elaine Lee, Iyko Day, Monica White Ndounou, Roderick Ferguson, Kymberly Newberry, Michael Boyce Gillespie, Vievee Francis, Thy Phu, Karilyn Crockett, Amanda Russhell Wallace, Aneeka Henderson, Jyoti Puri, Nikki A. Greene (girl, girl), Gail Lewis, Dell Marie Hamilton, K. Melchor Quick Hall, Kaysha Corinealdi, Marcia Chatelain, Nicole N. Ivy, and Patricia Ann Lott (the great Leo-sister): Thank you for your presence and the gift of your friendship. To my siblings: Shanesa, Yolanda, Bryan, Norman, Lyonel, Winston, Grace, and Oliver—I thank you for your unrelenting dedication to all things joyous. I thank Silvia Atilano and Ivelisse Viruet for everything they do that helps me to be who I am in the world.

And of course, to the women of the Dark Room: Race and Visual Culture Studies Seminar, I give my abiding thanks for conversations that have enlivened and enriched my thinking over the past decade. I would be nowhere without the grounding in visual culture you have helped me to sustain over the years.

To the artists examined in this book, I offer my deepest thanks: Roy DeCarava, Carrie Mae Weems, Ross Gay, Jennie C. Jones, Vievee Francis, Ibeyi, Carolina Chocolate Drops, Saidiya Hartman, Dell Marie Hamilton, Calida Rawles, Audre Lorde, John Coltrane, Michelle Cliff, Kahlil Joseph, Toby Sisson, Toni Morrison, Lucille Clifton, Steve McQueen, Jeannette Ehlers, Robert Hayden, Amanda Russhell Wallace, Gwendolyn Brooks, Barry Jenkins, Marvin Gaye, Sweet Honey in the Rock, Carl Phillips, Rebecca Hall, Toni Cade Bambara, James Baldwin, Jesmyn Ward, Alice Smith, and Mary Lee Bendolph: without you, nothing.

There was once a librarian in Throggs Neck who allowed nine-year-old me to drift over to the adult side of the library (you had to be at least twelve years old to visit without a parent or guardian). I was on the hunt for a Judy Blume novel. I found a book of black poetry. My life has never been the same.

To my father, Harold "Sylvester" Brown, I owe many things. Here, I want to thank him for his profound empathy and humanity. And the way he sees the gem of goodness in every endeavor, from gardening to curating music.

And lastly,

For humor, for art, for music (forever), for excess, abundance, for faith, for joy, for we who *"do language,"* for the senses and the sound, for poetry, for fury, for each and for every, for sun and for sea, for us, for us, for us, for we.

NOTES

INTRODUCTION

1. Thomas DeFrantz, *Dancing Revelations: Alvin Ailey's Embodiment of African American Culture* (Oxford: Oxford University Press, 2006), 6.

2. DeFrantz, *Dancing Revelations*, 4.

3. "Celebrating *Revelations* at 50," 2010, New Jersey Performing Arts Center, https://www.youtube.com/watch?v=44nqeAXLS-k.

4. Paul Gilroy, *The Black Atlantic: Modernity and Double Consciousness* (Oxford: Oxford University Press, 1993), 78.

5. Ren Ellis Neyra, *The Cry of the Senses: Listening to Latinx and Caribbean Poetics* (Raleigh, NC: Duke University Press, 2020), 58.

6. James Baldwin, *Notes of a Native Son* (Boston: Beacon Press, 1955), 41–42.

7. Elliott H. Powell, *Sounds from the Other Side: Afro-South Asian Collaborations in Black Popular Music* (Minneapolis: University of Minnesota Press, 2020), 27.

8. Baldwin, *Notes of a Native Son*, 85.

9. Baldwin, 88.

10. Baldwin, 113.

11. Raoul Peck, dir., *I Am Not Your Negro* (Magnolia Pictures, 2016).

12. Tiya Miles, *Tales from the Haunted South: Dark Tourism and Memories of Slavery from the Civil War Era* (Chapel Hill: University of North Carolina Press, 2015), 21.

13. Teju Cole, *Black Paper: Writing in a Dark Time* (Chicago: University of Chicago Press, 2021), 173.

14. Toni Morrison writes, "All water has a perfect memory and is forever trying to get back to where it was." From Morrison, "The Site of Memory," in *The Source of Self-Regard: Selected Essays, Speeches, and Meditations* (New York: Knopf, 2019), 243.

15. Morrison, "The Foreigner's House," in *The Source of Self-Regard*, 106; emphasis in original.

16. Habiba Ibrahim, *Black Age: Oceanic Lifespans and the Time of Black Life* (New York: New York University Press, 2021), 183.

17. Gwendolyn Brooks, "The Last Quatrain of the Ballad of Emmett Till," in *Blacks* (Chicago: Third World Press, 2000), 340.

18. Michael S. Harper, *Dear John, Dear Coltrane* (Urbana and Chicago: University of Illinois Press, 1970), 75.

19. Brooks, "The Last Quatrain of the Ballad of Emmett Till," 340.

20. Christina Sharpe, *In the Wake: On Blackness and Being* (Durham, NC: Duke University Press, 2016), 106; emphasis added.

21. Okwui Enwezor, *Grief and Grievance: Art and Mourning in America* (New York: Phaidon Press, 2020), 7.

22. Saidiya Hartman, *Lose Your Mother: A Journey Along the Atlantic Slave Route* (New York: Farrar, Strauss and Giroux, 2007), 5.

23. Toni Morrison's novel *Sula* ends with Nel's realization that she had for all those years been missing her friend. Her resulting cry "had no bottom and it had no top, just circles and circles of sorrow." Morrison, *Sula* (New York: Knopf, 1973), 174; emphasis added.

CHAPTER 1

1. Letter from Alvin Borgquist to W. E. B. Du Bois, April 11, 1905, University of Massachusetts at Amherst, https://credo.library.umass.edu/cgi-bin/pdf.cgi?id=scua:mums312-b001-i301; emphasis added.

2. Tina Campt, *Listening to Images* (Durham, NC: Duke University Press, 2016), 6.

3. Charles Rowell, "I Have Never Looked Back Since": An Interview with Roy DeCarava, *Callaloo* 13, no. 4 (Autumn 1990): 864.

4. Rowell, "I Have Never Looked Back Since," 864.

5. Toni Morrison, *Jazz* (New York: Vintage Books, 1992), 6.

6. Roland Barthes, *Camera Lucida* (New York: Hill and Wang, 1980), 9.

7. Morrison, *Jazz*, 12.

8. Morrison, 12.

9. Morrison, 3.

10. Toni Morrison, foreword to *Jazz*, xv.

11. Morrison, *Jazz*, 71.

12. Martin Luther King Jr., "Eulogy for the Young Victims," n.d., https://vimeo.com/34762047.

13. Sharpe, *In the Wake*, 17.

14. King, "Eulogy for the Young Victims."

15. Campt, *Listening to Images*, 107.

16. Randy Kennedy, "Roy DeCarava, Harlem Insider Who Photographed Ordinary Life, Dies at 89," *New York Times*, October 28, 2009.

17. Darby English, *How to See a Work of Art in Total Darkness* (Cambridge, MA: MIT Press, 2007), 6.

18. John Berger, *About Looking* (New York: Pantheon Books, 1980), 50.

19. Morrison, *Jazz*, 206.

20. Morrison, 226.

21. John Tagg, *The Disciplinary Frame: Photographic Truths and the Capture of Meaning* (Minneapolis: University of Minnesota Press, 2009), 1.

22. Ivor Miller, "If It Hasn't Been One of Color": An Interview with Roy DeCarava," *Callaloo* 13, no. 4 (Autumn 1990): 851.

23. Rowell, "I Have Never Looked Back Since," 871.

24. Faith Smith, *Strolling in the Ruins: The Caribbean's Non-Sovereign Modern in the Early Twentieth Century* (Durham, NC: Duke University Press, 2023), 8.

25. Jessica Lanay, "To Know Your Family So Specifically: Jeannette Ehlers Interviewed," *BOMB* Magazine, December 14, 2021, 4, https://bombmagazine.org/articles/2021/12/14/to-know-your-family-so-specifically-jeannette-ehlers-interviewed/.

26. Robert Hayden's poem "Frederick Douglass" refers to "freedom" as "this beautiful and terrible thing, / needful to man as air." Hayden, *Collected Poems* (New York: Liveright Publishing Corporation, 1985), 62.

27. Sault, "I Am Free," 2022, https://www.youtube.com/watch?v=C44BAmw1K5k.

28. Sault, *Untitled (God)* (Forever Living Originals, 2022); Jeannette Ehlers, *Black Bullets* (video still), 2012.

29. In a text message to the author from March 2023, Sisson wrote: "There is so much connection across time and place . . . the Black Tears continue to surface again and again."

30. James Baldwin, *I Am Not Your Negro* (New York: Vintage International, 2016), viii. A companion edition to the documentary film directed by Raoul Peck and based on texts by Baldwin.

31. Baldwin with Peck, *I Am Not Your Negro*, x.

32. James Baldwin, *The Devil Finds Work* (New York: Vintage International, 2011), 6–7.

33. Baldwin, *The Devil Finds Work*, 6–7.

34. Baldwin, 64.

35. Baldwin with Peck, *I Am Not Your Negro*, 47.

36. James Baldwin, *The Fire Next Time* (New York: Vintage International, 1992), 7.

37. Baldwin, *The Fire Next Time*, 7.

38. Baldwin, 33.

39. Roland Barthes, *Camera Lucida*, 39.

40. Baldwin, *The Fire Next Time*, 104; emphasis added.

41. Baldwin, 104–105.

42. Glenn Ligon's 2000 screenprint *Untitled (Crowd/The Fire Next Time)* uses Baldwin's poignant question as the framework of his layered meditation on the Million Man March, which took place in Washington, DC, in 1995.

43. Baldwin with Peck, *I Am Not Your Negro*, 12.

44. Trica Keaton, *You Know You're Black in France When: The Fact of Everyday Antiblackness* (Cambridge, MA: MIT Press, 2023), 10.

45. Terence Dixon, dir., *Meeting the Man: James Baldwin in Paris* (Buzzy Enterprises, 1970).

46. Baldwin with Peck, *I Am Not Your Negro?*, 13–14.

47. Toni Cade Bambara, *Gorilla, My Love* (New York: First Vintage Contemporaries Edition, 1992), 99.

48. Bambara, *Gorilla, My Love*, 99.

49. Bambara, 111.

50. Bambara, 100.

51. Bambara, 100.

52. Bambara, 112; emphasis in original.

53. Juliet Hooker, *Black Grief, White Grievance: The Politics of Loss* (Princeton, NJ: Princeton University Press, 2023), 201.

54. Bambara, *Gorilla, My Love*, 102.

55. Bambara, 111–112.

56. Bambara, 101.

57. Campt, *Listening to Images*, 107.

58. Judith Jamison quoted in "*Cry*," https://www.alvinailey.org/performances/repertory/cry.

59. DeFrantz, *Dancing Revelations*, 184.

60. Lucille Clifton, *Quilting: Poems* (New York: BOA Editions, Ltd., 1991), 17.

CHAPTER 2

1. Steve McQueen, *Ashes*, 2002–2015, https://vimeo.com/127652956.

2. Harper's first book of poetry, *Dear John, Dear Coltrane*, was published in 1970. The title poem was written in 1966, just a year before Coltrane's unexpected death. It functions as an elegy for the musician and is often presented as such.

3. In a Yahoo Entertainment! Interview, Coogler discusses writing dialogue for Boseman, words the actor would never utter on-screen

because of his untimely death. https://www.youtube.com/watch?v=A5SqFLKfby8.

4. Lucille Clifton, *Blessing the Boats: New and Selected Poems 1988–2000* (New York: BOA Editions, Ltd, 2000), 82.

5. Named Operation Urgent Fury, the United States military invades Grenada, claiming the Marxist regime in power is a threat to the nearly one thousand American citizens on the small Caribbean island. See https://www.youtube.com/watch?v=bW2_vmJdJ24.

6. Dionne Brand, *Map to the Door of No Return: Notes to Belonging* (Toronto: Vintage Canada, 2001), 158.

7. Campt, *Listening to Images*, 2.

8. Campt, 6.

9. Having visited Jones's monument on two different occasions, I may have been one of the unlucky few who didn't have an atmospheric assist. I failed to hear anything either time. But this silence was also instructive, for it compelled me to attend to what I did hear in the light subtlety of sun and the stillness of the wind.

10. Karla FC Holloway, *Passed On: African American Mourning Stories: A Memorial* (Durham, NC: Duke University Press, 2003), 57.

11. Huey Copeland, "First Takes: A Conversation with Jennie C. Jones," in *Compilation*, ed. Jennie C. Jones (Houston: Gregory R. Miller & Co., 2015), 25.

12. W. E. B. Du Bois, *The Souls of Black Folk* (Scotts Valley, CA: CreateSpace Independent Publishing Platform, 2014), 97.

13. Du Bois, *The Souls of Black Folk*, 98.

14. Karla FC Holloway, *Passed On: African American Mourning Stories: A Memorial* (Durham, NC: Duke University Press, 2003), 7.

15. Alexander Weheliye, *Phonographies: Grooves in Sonic Afro-Modernity* (Durham, NC: Duke University Press, 2005), 85.

16. I. Augustus Durham, *Stay Black and Die: On Melancholy and Genius* (Durham, NC: Duke University Press, 2023), 119.

17. Amiri Baraka (Leroi Jones), *Blues People: Negro Music in White America* (New York: Harper Perennial, 1999), 17.

18. Robert Hayden, "Frederick Douglass," *Collected Poems*, ed. Frederick Glaysher (New York: Liveright Books, 1985), 62.

19. Baldwin, *The Fire Next Time*, 42.

20. Vievee Francis, *The Shared World: Poems* (Evanston, IL: Northwestern University Press, 2023), 50; emphasis in original.

21. Francis, *The Shared World*, 41.

22. Shana Redmond, *Anthem: Social Movements and the Sound of Solidarity in the African Diaspora* (New York: New York University Press, 2013), 11.

23. Ross Gay, "A Small Needful Fact," Split This Rock, *The Quarry: A Social Justice Poetry Database*, 2015, https://www.splitthisrock.org/poetry-database/poem/a-small-needful-fact--this one should work. Split This Rock is a DC-based art center.

24. Jesmyn Ward, *Salvage the Bones* (New York: Bloomsbury, 2011), 14.

25. Matthew D. Morrison, *Blacksound: Making Race and Popular Music in the United States* (Oakland, CA: University of California Press, 2024), 91.

26. W. E. B. Du Bois, *The Souls of Black Folk* (New York: Barnes and Noble Classics, 2003), 177.

27. Robert Burns Stepto, *A Home Elsewhere: Reading African American Classics in the Age of Obama* (Cambridge, MA: Harvard University Press, 2010), 142–144.

28. Saidiya Hartman, *Lose Your Mother: A Journey Along the Atlantic Slave Route* (New York: Farrar, Straus and Giroux, 2007), 108.

29. Michelle Cliff, *No Telephone to Heaven* (New York: Plume, 1987), 7, 12.

30. Cliff writes, "The grandmother was long since dead, and the farm had been left by the family to the forest. To *ruination*, the grandmother would have said. The family, but one, were scattered through America and England and had begun new lives, some transplanted for more than twenty years, and no one wanted to return and reclaim the property—at least not until now." New nations and hegemonic forces pulled Claire's lineage off the land. She returns as an adult to connect her body to her familial space. Cliff, *No Telephone to Heaven*, 8.

31. Faith Smith, *Strolling Through the Ruins: The Caribbean's Non-sovereign Modern in the Early Twentieth Century* (Durham, NC: Duke University Press, 2023), 26.

32. Cliff, 10.

33. Giuliana Bruno, *Public Intimacy: Architecture and the Visual Arts* (Cambridge, MA: MIT Press, 2007), 82.

34. Published the same year as Toni Morrison's *Beloved, No Telephone to Heaven* similarly utilizes the alliterative properties of doubling and repetition (Clare/Clear, Harry/Harriet). The character of Christopher, living on the jagged edges of a hypermarginal existence, uses the landscape as a form of retreat, and having been born and raised without the benefit of home and parental interaction, Christopher functions as a symbolic martyr (*St. Christopher*) to Jamaican nationalism.

35. Saidiya Hartman, "Venus in Two Acts," *Small Axe* 26 (June 2008): 10, https://read.dukeupress.edu/small-axe/article-pdf/12/2/1/503379/2-sa26+hartman+(1-14).pdf.

36. Lauret Savoy, *Trace: Memory, History, Race, and the American Landscape* (Berkeley: Counterpoint Books, 2015), 92.

37. Thomas Jefferson, *Notes on the State of Virginia* (Chapel Hill: University of North Carolina Press, 1954), 139.

38. Sharpe, *In the Wake*, 114.

39. According to the Whitney Plantation website, "Whitney Institute educates the public about the history and legacies of slavery in the United States." In this declaration, it differs from many other plantation sites throughout the north and south that treat slavery as accidental or nonexistent. See http://whitneyplantation.org.

40. Ren Ellis Neyra, *The Cry of the Senses: Listening to Latinx and Caribbean Poetics* (Durham, NC: Duke University Press, 2020), 134.

41. Neyra, *Cry of the Senses*, 130.

42. Saidiya Hartman, *Lose Your Mother: A Journey Along the Atlantic Slave Route* (New York: Farrar, Straus and Giroux, 2007), 108.

43. Warsan Shire, "What They Did Yesterday Afternoon," https://verse.press/poem/what-they-did-yesterday-afternoon-6524900794187889060.

44. Hartman, *Lose Your Mother*, 70.

45. "I am the name of the sound and the sound of the name" is from "Thunder, Perfect Mind," by The Nag Hammadi.

46. Hartman, *Lose Your Mother*, 137.

47. Hartman, 136.

48. Hartman, 138.

49. Amanda Russhell Wallace, *Mo(u)rning Tea, Extracted*, 2011, https://www.amandarwallace.com/time-based.

50. Michael Boyce Gillespie, *Film Blackness: American Cinema and the Idea of Black Film* (Durham, NC: Duke University Press, 2016), 7.

51. The conversation between Joseph and Jafa is located here: https://www.youtube.com/watch?v=otPECh1Q2xQ.

52. Hilton Als, "The Black Excellence of Kahlil Joseph," *New Yorker*, October 30, 2017, https://www.newyorker.com/magazine/2017/11/06/the-black-excellence-of-kahlil-joseph.

CHAPTER 3

1. Michael Boyce Gillespie, "One Step Ahead: A Conversation with Barry Jenkins," *Film Quarterly* 70, no. 3: 55.

2. James Laxton, "The Photographic Inspirations Behind *Moonlight*, 2016's Best Picture," interview by Andrew Strecker, November 21, 2023, https://www.lensculture.com/articles/moonlight-cinematography-the-photographic-inspirations-behind-moonlight-2016-s-best-picture.

3. bell hooks, "The Oppositional Gaze: Black Female Spectators," in *Feminism and Visual Culture Reader*, ed. Amelia Jones (New York: Routledge, 2002), 94.

4. Barry Jenkins, dir., *Moonlight* (A24 / Plan B Entertainment, 2016).

5. Michael Boyce Gillespie, "One Step Ahead," 54.

6. Jafari Allen, *There's a Disco Ball Between Us: A Theory of Black Gay Life* (Durham, NC: Duke University Press, 2022), 71; emphasis in original.

7. Kevin Quashie, *Black Aliveness, Or a Poetics of Being* (Durham, NC: Duke University Press, 2021), 23.

8. Michael Boyce Gillespie, "One Step Ahead," 56.

9. Carl Phillips, *Silverchest* (New York: Farrar, Straus and Giroux, 2013), 56.

10. Morrison, *Jazz*, 60.

11. Morrison, 61.

12. Morrison, 65.

13. Audre Lorde, *Zami: A New Spelling of My Name: A Biomythography* (New York: Random House, 1982), 97.

14. Amber Jamilla Musser, *Sensual Excess: Queer Femininity and Brown Jouissance* (New York: New York University Press, 2018), 175–176.

15. Baldwin, *The Fire Next Time*, 43.

16. James Elkins, *The Object Stares Back* (New York: HarperOne, 1997), 210.

17. Nella Larsen, *Passing: A Norton Critical Edition*, ed. Carla Kaplan (New York: W. W. Norton & Company, 2007), 6.

18. Rebecca Hall, dir., *Passing* (Picture Films / Netflix Studios, 2021).

19. Michèle Pearson Clarke, "A Dark Horse in Low Light," 6.

20. Allen, *There's a Disco Ball Between Us*, 198.

21. Allen, 263.

22. Transcription: *People of a Darker Hue*, 2016, McMullenMuseum.bc.edu, https://mcmullenmuseum.bc.edu/exhibitions/weems/transcriptios/people.html.

23. LaCharles Ward, "'Keep Runnin' Bro': Carrie Mae Weems and the Visual Act of Refusal," *Black Camera* 9, no. 2 (Spring 2018): 82–109, 98.

24. Transcription: *People of a Darker Hue*, 2016.

25. Morrison, *Jazz*, 229; emphasis in original.

CODA

1. Dionne Brand, *A Map to the Door of No Return: Notes to Belonging* (Toronto: Vintage Canada, 2001), 8.

2. Brand, *A Map to the Door of No Return*, 7.

3. Joseph Roach, *Cities of the Dead: Circum-Atlantic Performance* (New York: Columbia University Press, 1996), 69.

INDEX